By John H. Auble

SAINT LOUIS

Contents

Series Editors: Thomas J. Doyle and Rodney L. Rathmann

Write to the Library for the Blind, 1333 S. Kirkwood Road, St. Louis, MO 63122-7295 to obtain this study in braille or large print for the visually impaired.

Introduction

The Godly Man Series

In his letter to the recently established Christian church at Philippi, the apostle Paul likened the Christian life to a race. Paul wrote, "Forgetting what is behind and straining toward what is ahead, I press on toward the goal to win the prize for which God has called me heavenward in Christ Jesus" (Philippians 3:13–14).

Each of us who by faith claims Jesus as Lord and Savior has God's permission and His power to forget "what is behind." Over 2,000 years ago, Jesus came to earth, true God, Son of the eternal Father and yet True Man. Conceived by the Holy Spirit and born of the Virgin Mary, Jesus grew as a boy—through childhood and adolescence—to become a mature man. He endured all the temptations and struggles every man has faced and yet committed no sin of thought, word, or action (see Hebrews 4:14–15). According to His Father's plan, He suffered and died on the cross as our substitute, taking our sins upon Himself. We can forget our sins because Jesus' love has overcome our past. He has won the victory over our sins and the constraining, handicapping power of the devil. Jesus showed Himself Lord over sin, death, and the devil when He rose from the dead on Easter morning. We who believe in the crucified, risen, and ascended Savior are made new men by the same Holy Spirit who brought us to faith. As God's Spirit gives us new desires and a new set of goals and priorities, He changes us through the Word of God—the Gospel—so that we come to know God's love and the outpouring of His grace in mighty ways, and grow in our relationship with our Father in heaven. Long ago, the psalmist wrote by inspiration of the Holy Spirit the following insight into God and His nature, "His pleasure is not in the strength of the horse, nor His delight in the legs of man; the LORD delights in those who fear Him, who put their hope in His unfailing love" (Psalm 147:10–11).

As we run life's race, our heavenly Father invites us to find our strength and encouragement in Him. His joy is not in any physical means by which men may reach a finish line, such as in the power of a horse or the legs of men. Rather, God finds His joy in those sons who put their hope in Him and in the power of His unfailing love.

God's Word reminds us, "[We] are all sons of God through faith in Christ Jesus" (Galatians 3:26) and our God delights in His relationship with His sons just as every good father prides himself in the growth and accomplishments of his children. He invites us to communicate with Him regularly and often as we experience His Word and respond to His love in prayer.

As we press on toward our heavenly prize, God helps us to live our lives for Him. Many of God's faithful people, both men and women, have lived it before us. Theirs is a heritage for us to build upon and to pass on to those who will follow after us— our wives, children, friends, and others whose lives will be touched by the love and power of God evidenced in our lives.

The writer to the Hebrews encourages us to live as men of faith, reminding us about where to keep our focus as we run life's race: "Therefore, since we are surrounded by such a great cloud of witnesses, let us throw off everything that hinders and the sin that so easily entangles, and let us run with perseverance the race marked out for us. Let us fix our eyes on Jesus, the author and perfecter of our faith, who for the joy set before Him endured the cross, scorning its shame, and sat down at the right hand of the throne of God. Consider Him who endured such opposition from sinful men, so that you will not grow weary and lose heart" (Hebrews 12:1–3).

God's blessings as you run the race and claim the prize already won for you!

About the Godly Man Series

The Godly Man series is especially for men. Written in book-study format, each course in the Godly Man series is organized into chapters suitable for either group or individual study. Periodically throughout each chapter, questions have been provided to further stimulate your thinking, assist you in personal application, and spark group discussion.

How to Use Each Course in the Godly Man Series

Each course in the Godly Man series has been prepared especially for small group settings. It may, however, be used as a self-study or in a traditional Sunday morning Bible class. Chapters of each course may be read in advance of group discussion. Or participants may take turns reading sections of the Bible study during your group study sessions.

Planning for a Small Group Study

1. *Select a leader* for the course or a leader for the day. It will be the leader's responsibility to secure needed materials, to keep the discussion moving, and to help involve all participants.

2. *Emphasize sharing.* Your class will work best if the participants feel comfortable with one another and if all feel their contributions to the class are important and useful. Take the necessary time at the beginning of the course to get to know one another. Since this course deals with relationship issues, you may ask participants to share their names and a little something about a positive relationship they have now or have had in the past. Share what you expect to gain from this course. Develop an atmosphere of openness, trust, and caring among the participants. Agree in advance that private issues shared during your study will remain within the group.

3. *Pray for one another.* Begin and conclude each study session with a prayer. Pray for one another, for your families, your work, and all other aspects of your life. Involve everyone. Consider praying-around-the-circle, with each person offering a specific prayer to God for the person on his left.

As You Plan to Lead the Group

1. Read this guide in its entirety before you lead the first session.

2. Use the Answers and Comments section in the back of the study.

3. Pray each day for those in your group.

4. Depend on the Holy Spirit. Expect His presence; He will guide you and cause you to grow. God will not let His Word return empty (see Isaiah 55:11) as you study it individually or with others in a group.

5. Prepare well, studying each session's material thoroughly. Add your comments in the margins so that you may add your insights to spark conversation and discussion throughout the session.

6. Begin and end the session with prayer.

7. Begin and end on time. Punctuality is a courtesy to everyone and can be a factor to encourage discussion.

8. Find ways to keep the session informal; consider meeting over breakfast at a local restaurant or some other friendly setting where participants can be seated face to face.

9. Keep the class moving. Limit your discussion to questions of interest to the participants. Be selective. You don't need to cover every question. Note that most Bible references are included in the study guide. At times, however, you may want to look up and share additional insights provided by other suggested Bible references.

10. Build one another up through your fellowship and study. Make a conscious effort to support one another in your personal and professional challenges.

Expect and rejoice in God's presence and blessing as He builds your faith and enriches your life through the study of His Word.

FindinG MeaninG and Purpose

Two Tragedies

Mark Mitchell checked his watch. A midnight flight. The local radio tower crew had gone home for the evening. He could either stay in touch with a nearby airfield, or remain on his own.

He chose to fly on his own. He was no novice. After all, he'd had his pilot's license for more than two years. He'd flown after hours like this before. Many times. But tonight he had more on his mind than practicing his flying skills.

He started the engine. The droning, familiar noise failed to penetrate the depths of his thoughts. He taxied down the runway and took off, flying east to west.

What would they say at work tomorrow, he wondered. Now they would finally have something to talk about besides his financial indiscretions. They had elected him three times to public office; how could it come to this?

Reaching the altitude of 400 feet, he leveled off. Not noticing the bright, twinkling city lights beneath him, he paused for a minute. In his mind, he raced through the recent events that had suddenly turned his world upside down. He silently studied each one, trying somehow to make sense of it all. Was he doing the right thing? Had his life come down to this one defining moment?

And then, without hesitating, he pushed the throttle in with the nose of his plane pointed downward. He accelerated perpendicular to the ground, propelled by gravity and the power of his plane. One last thought that entered his mind was the darkness. It was so dark, he might not even see the ground coming before impact.

And so, a young man ended his own life at over 100 m.p.h. with a sickening thud into the earth and a final, engulfing cloud of debris and dust. In the end Mark Mitchell, a celebrity, one who was well known by so many had to be identified by his dental records.

On the night of Mark's suicide, Demetrius Lamont sat by himself in the southcity apartment he had shared with his girlfriend. He too faced the lonely darkness. His eyes stared unfocused on the hazy gray outside his window. Alone with his broken dreams and disappointments, Demetrius found suddenly that he missed Shantae.

Demetrius thought about how much he had wanted to be Shantae's husband. In their happy times, they had talked together about their baby and about the family life they would share. Demetrius wanted to be a loving husband, and he wanted to be a good father. He had watched young fathers together with their children in the park. He knew he would be the best of dads though he never had a father of his own. In his mind, Demetrius had seen himself and Shantae playing with their baby—a boy—in their apartment, in the park, and at family gatherings. But these dreams had been his, not Shantae's. Now they weren't even his.

If only Shantae would come back. Then they could start over and build their dreams again, one by one. But she wasn't coming back and he knew it. In a fit of anger and spite, she had ended the life of their unborn child. And then just as finally, she had ended their relationship.

Demetrius had grown up in the city—the urban jungle, but tonight he didn't feel so tough. Wounded with Shantae's invisible knife, he wondered if he could ever be the same again. At least I have my job, he consoled himself. What will I tell them at work when they ask about Shantae ... and our baby.

React and Respond

1. Someone once said, "There are three aspects of every man: who he thinks he is, who others think he is, and who he really is. Do you agree or disagree? Explain.

2. Both Mark and Demetrius saw their worlds crumble down around them. They were broken men, broken in heart and crushed in spirit. Like Judas Iscariot, who betrayed our

Lord, Mark and Demetrius faced despair and helplessness. Mark ended his life. Neither Mark nor Demetrius realized that man's failure is God's opportunity. God specializes in restoring brokenness. Himself once a broken man, David confidently professed, "a broken and contrite heart, O God, You will not despise" (Psalm 51:17). It was to rebuild lives broken by sin that God sent His Son to live a perfect life and die a torturous death in our place.

a. Have you ever known tragic stories like those of Mark Mitchell or Demetrius Lamont?

b. What potential for similar tragedies do you see in those of your acquaintance?

c. When was the last time you felt broken by sin?

3. Explain the meaning of the following for all who are grieved and oppressed by the weight of their sin:

> Man's failure is God's opportunity.
> He does not remember sweet things who has not tasted bitter.
> Wash me, and I will be whiter than snow. Psalm 51:7b

4. What part could we play to keep the tragedy of Mark Mitchell from repeating itself in our lives or the lives of those we know?

5. What could you do or say to help Demetrius if you were his close friend?

You've experienced it before. A room full of strangers. The room is thick with the silent awkwardness of meeting and finding out about other people. The inevitability of "The Question" hangs over everyone's head. It's always one of the first, if not the first, questions asked, "So, what do you do for a living?"

When someone asks you what you do for a living, do you wish "The Question" had never been asked? Or maybe you're just the opposite. Perhaps you feel a real sense of pride when you get to share the details of your occupation with someone. In social situations you may even ask others "The Question" so they might feel obligated and ask you the same. Do you feel a burst of pride when you blurt out, "I'm a college professor with several published works," or "I work in the automotive industry. Right now we are making minivans."

"The Question" takes on such meaning and significance because so many of us see it as a first step in knowing and understanding others. And yet, does what we do for a living really say that much about who we are? To what extent do we define ourselves by what we do for a living?

Does a man's type of employment or lack of employment accurately measure his worth as a human being? Maybe in society's eyes. But fortunately for us, not in God's eyes. Even though they are looking at the same subject, God's eyes see something altogether different than man's.

1 Samuel 16:1–13 tells how God taught the Old Testament prophet Samuel a lesson about judging others. God sent Samuel to Jesse to anoint one of his sons as the new king of the people of Israel. Before Samuel arrived, the Lord had already chosen one of Jesse's sons.

When Samuel saw the first of Jesse's sons (who happened to be big, strong, and handsome), he immediately thought to himself, "This looks like the one to me. He's tall and good looking. Yep. This has got to be the one." But God quickly told him, "Nope. You're wrong. And the reason you're wrong is you are quick to judge things by their outward appearance. I don't judge things the way you do." In a sense, He was saying people cannot be fairly judged when the contents of their hearts are not taken into account. That's why everyone should be slow to judge anyone. What's in our hearts is more important than our outward appearance or someone's opinion of us. The inner condition of our hearts defines us best.

By man's standards, David would have been the last one selected as king or ruler. In fact, Jesse was so sure David wouldn't be chosen that he didn't even think it was necessary to invite him to Samuel's sacrificial ceremony. By man's standards, David was unqualified and insignificant. He's just a young man tending his father's sheep. It doesn't take a college education to tend to sheep. You don't exactly have to be strong to excel in shepherding either. But here was David faithfully and unquestioningly doing his humble duty.

Nevertheless, by God's standards, David was THE man. It was what was in David's heart that made him acceptable. It was his faith. God completely searches a person's heart. God is the only judge who can get a clear, fair, and true definition of any person.

God doesn't need to define us by what we do or how we earn a living. He regard's a man's work as what it truly is—only a partial, transient part of the whole person. The whole picture of a Christian includes an important, undeniable fact: By the power of the Spirit, because we belong to Christ, He actually dwells in us. Every day. Not just when we're doing good deeds. All the time. Romans 6:8 says:

> Now if we died with Christ, we believe that we will also live with Him. For we know that since Christ was raised from the dead, He cannot die again; death no longer has mastery over Him. The death He died, He died to sin once for all; but the life He lives, He lives to God.

Therefore, because of Christ and the life we have in and through Him, we are to live our lives to God. Employed by Him. Defined by Him.

1 Corinthians 7:23 says we were bought at a price. It took Jesus' suffering death on the cross. We therefore owe our very lives and existence to Him who redeemed us. Now by His power, we can live the rest of our lives as a thank You to God and what He has done for us in the saving work of His Son. Over the course of a lifetime, we can neither fully comprehend the depth of the love behind God's redeeming act nor even begin to repay it. A preacher once said, "Stop and think about

it for a minute; if you were the only person on earth, Jesus Christ would still go to the cross to suffer and die for you. He cared about you personally—that much!"

REACT AND RESPOND

1. Reflect a moment about "The Question." How do you feel when someone asks you "The Question"?

2. 2 Corinthians 5 describes the extent to which God went to give us true value through the sacrifice of His only Son for us on Calvary's cross, "God made Him who had no sin to be sin for us, so that in Him we might become the righteousness of God" (verse 21). The same chapter speaks about the difference Christ's love makes in a believers attitudes,

> For Christ's love compels us, because we are convinced that one died for all, and therefore all died. And He died for all, that those who live should no longer live for themselves but for Him who died for them and was raised again.
> So from now on we regard no one from a worldly point of view. Though we once regarded Christ in this way [according to the standards of the world], we do so no longer. Therefore, if anyone is in Christ, He is a new creation; the old has gone, the new has come! (2 Corinthians 5:14–17)

How does the newness you have in Christ affect the way you think about yourself? about others?

3. It's important to put our work into perspective. According to the following passage from Job, God sometimes inter-

venes, even through the use of natural forces, to divert a man's attention away from work to more important things. Read the passage then give one or two examples of times when God got your attention in a unique or significant way.

> God's voice thunders in marvelous ways; He does great things beyond our understanding. He says to the snow, "Fall on the earth," and to the rain shower, "Be a mighty downpour." So that all men He has made may know His work, He stops every man from his labor. (Job 37:5–7)

A View of Vocations

On our own none of us amount to very much. The Bible tells us, "All have sinned and fallen short of the glory of God." We are fortunate indeed that God measures us by who we are in Him in relation to His Son. Nothing more. Nothing less.

What would happen if God one day decided to measure us by our occupations—the same way the world measures us? Suppose that one day God, borrowing society's standards, decreed that it was too demeaning and demoralizing for people to be nurses. Nurses sometimes have to clean bedpans, many don't make much money, and the work they do really embarrasses Him. All nurses, God rules, must find new lines of work. The removal of nurses from society would be felt immediately. Someone must care for those who are sick and unable to care for themselves. One of the richest ironies of our world is that society could not function without people filling the occupations it tends to regard as insignificant.

Our God is a God of order. Our world needs people of a variety of talents and abilities in every occupation. And every honorable occupation can be done to the glory of God and for the benefit of society as a grateful response to God for all He has given us through Christ Jesus our Lord. Every person has a useful function he or she can perform.

For the encouragement of God's people, Paul writes, "Whatever you do, work at it with all your heart, as working for the Lord, not for men, since you know that you will receive an inheritance from the Lord as a reward. It is the Lord Christ you are serving" (Colossians 3:23–24). Paul's words remind us that we can dedicate each day's work to God, honoring Him with our best efforts, even though others may not appreciate or even notice our best efforts.

React and Respond

1. Before the fall into sin the first man lived in paradise. Even here God gave man work to do. Genesis 2:15 records, "The LORD God took the man and put him in the Garden of Eden to work it and take care of it." What good things does God bring to your life through the work He has given you to do?

2. Apply the following passage to the way God provides for society through the diversity of interests and occupations available within it.

> Now the body is not made up of one part but of many. If the foot should say, "Because I am not a hand, I do not belong to the body," it would not for that reason cease to be part of the body. And if the ear should say, "Because I am not an eye, I do not belong to the body," it would not for that reason cease to be part of the body. If the whole body were an eye, where would the sense of hearing be? If the whole body were an ear, where would the sense of smell be? But in fact God has arranged the parts in the body, every one of them, just as He wanted them to be. If they were all one part, where would the body be? As it is, there are many parts, but one body. (1 Corinthians 12:14–20)

Our Work, His Perspective

In Ecclesiastes, King Solomon, through the wisdom of God, shares his conclusions about life and labor. He notes in Ecclesiastes 2:10–11 that his heart delighted in his work, but it soon dawned on him that his joy was fleeting and temporal. This transient joy, in and of itself, was the only reward for all of his labor. Upon examining what had come of his efforts, he came to the grim realization that nothing was gained and his efforts were hopelessly futile. In Solomon's own words, he was chasing the wind when it came to finding meaning in his work without God.

Solomon also recognizes the importance of work and of enjoying the blessings of life which include a fulfilling and satisfying vocation. Solomon says, "A man can do nothing better than to eat and drink and find satisfaction in his work. This too, I see, is from the hand of God, for without Him, who can eat or find enjoyment?" (Ecclesiastes 2:24–25). Solomon adds that God also blesses His people through the labors of unbelievers, "To the man who pleases Him, God gives wisdom, knowledge and happiness, but to the sinner He gives the task of gathering and storing up wealth to hand it over to the one who pleases God" (Ecclesiastes 2:26).

God invites us to put *our* work into *His* perspective. Everything man puts his hands on eventually subsides. Everything God touches endures forever. It is immutable. God has a very special reason for clearly pointing out the differences between our work and His work:

> I know that everything God does will endure forever; nothing can be added to it and nothing taken from it. God does it so that men will revere Him. (Ecclesiastes 3:14)

Think about what you have waiting for you at work tomorrow. Do you have a big report due? Maybe you have a presentation you're not sure you're going to have prepared on time. What insurmountable problem has you scared about your work? Do you have a problem relationship with a boss or co-worker that you just don't know how to resolve? Or do you struggle with the monotony of doing the same old thing day in and day out?

Put your work-related concerns into perspective. Think about whatever it is about your problem at work that has stolen some of your sleep, caused you anxiety, made you lose your temper with loved ones and friends. Write it on a piece of paper. Pray about it, turning the matter over to God and asking Him to carry the burden of your struggle for you. Then put the paper away. Continue to bring the matter before the Lord in prayer. At the end of six months pull out the piece of paper and ask yourself if the problem you recorded six months earlier is still a concern. If it is, put the paper away and continue as before. In six months review the paper and consider the situation one more time. Accumulate the papers and keep them as a reminder. Thanks to the grace of our loving and caring God most of the things that trouble and concern us have no lasting importance or significance.

React and Respond

1. Share a situation where God has given something good to you through the efforts of someone who does not yet believe in Jesus as his or her Savior?

2. What eternal dimension can the power and presence of Christ bring to your work?

In Search of a True Definition

When we realize the futility of defining ourselves by something we do, touch, or accomplish and empty ourselves of any puffed-up notion of our self-sufficiency, a beautiful thing happens. Just when we realize and begin to comprehend the hopelessness and depths of our situation, God steps in to remind us of our place in His kingdom as adopted children. We are therefore defined by who we are in Christ, whose real work (the only important work as far as we're concerned) is the only work that matters because it endures forever.

When we are defined by Christ's love, by the gift of faith, everything in our lives eminates from this central, liberating truth. Because Jesus is Lord of our lives, we are free to live our lives fulfilled and content as the redeemed people He has made us to be. As Christians, we are constrained by the love of Christ. That is, the love of God shown through the sacrificial work of His Son is so real to us that we are captivated by it. Literally, we are prisoners of Christ's love, forever contained within its soft yet firm grip. We can do nothing outside of it. It will not let go of us. This is the true definition of who we are.

For as we are reconciled to God through Christ, we become Christ's ambassadors. So then, this is our career. It is our full-time occupation. Our reason for jumping out of bed in anticipation of each new day no matter what we do for a living.

React and Respond

1. How does the following passage from Psalms help us as Christian men to keep our work in perspective?

> He makes grass grow for the cattle, and plants for man to cultivate—bringing forth food from the earth. (Psalm 104:14)

2. Read Psalm 1, printed below as your closing. How does God's power enter into the lives of those who "do not walk in the counsel of the wicked or stand in the way of sinners or sit in the seat of mockers?" What examples can you recognize of God watching over your way in your work or private life?

> Blessed is the man who does not walk in the counsel of the wicked or stand in the way of sinners or sit in the seat of mockers. But his delight is in the law of the LORD, and on His law he meditates day and night. He is like a tree planted by streams of water, which yields its fruit in season and whose leaf does not wither. Whatever he does prospers.
>
> Not so the wicked! They are like chaff that the wind blows away. Therefore the wicked will not stand in the judgment, nor sinners in the assembly of the righteous.
>
> For the LORD watches over the way of the righteous, but the way of the wicked will perish.

2 | Finding Time

Slip sliding away.

Bob glanced over his shoulder at the calendar that hung from the wall. "Great," he thought to himself, "this report was due last week, and I'm just now getting to it. What's my boss going to say?"

Bob quickly reviewed the last two weeks trying to figure out what happened. Had he missed an opportunity, some free time he could have used to do the report? He couldn't think of one spare moment. It's not because I'm a slacker, he thought.

If there were slackers in the company, Bob wasn't one of them. He worked hard, putting in a lot of overtime. Bob remembered once commenting half-jokingly to a colleague, "If I figured out how many hours I actually spend doing my job, I'd bet my salary would work out to be minimum wage."

While Bob was working on the report, his secretary, Margaret, came in with 12 phone messages.

"Twelve?" he said to Margaret with an underlying tone of both frustration and disbelief.

"Hey, I don't make them, I just write them down."

"Yeah, okay. Thanks, Margaret." Margaret quietly left the room unaware of any burden she'd just placed there.

No sooner had she left then Sandy and Alex came in.

"What are you doing, Bob?" Sandy asked, not waiting for an answer. "The designers are waiting in the corner conference room. We were supposed to start the meeting 10 minutes ago, remember? Let's go."

Bob wondered how the day had gotten away from him so quickly. He was deep in his own thoughts as he left his office for the meeting. So deep, he didn't notice his computer beeping.

Someone was trying to send him another urgent e-mail message. It was his fifth one that day.

Driving home, Bob planned the few hours he had for his

personal life. He hadn't been spending much time with his children lately. Maybe they could watch a movie together. Then he remembered. Tonight was Tuesday, his evangelism group met on Tuesday nights.

Evangelism was something Bob felt God had called him to do. He knew it was important. He felt strongly that Christians owed it to God to tithe time and talents in addition to treasures, so he regularly gave God a generous portion of his time.

Bob's wife, Marla, would have to tend to the children tonight. He wouldn't be back until late. Bob felt Marla understood and agreed with him on the importance of his work with the evangelism group. When he gave of his time to the Lord, he dedicated it to God, but he also gave of his time on behalf of his whole family. "I'll tithe the time to God for me and for my family," he had decided.

When he got home, his five-year-old son went through the same routine as always. He hid behind the doorway in the darkness, anxiously awaiting his unsuspecting dad. When Bob came in, Josh greeted him with the usual, "Raaaaaaaaarrrrrrrrrrrrrhhhhhhhh!!!!!!"

But this time, his dad didn't play along as he usually did. He didn't fall to the ground out of psuedoshock. He didn't clutch his chest melodramatrically and fall backward, acting as if he were having a heart attack. He wasn't startled. He didn't even act scared or surprised.

Instead, his dad leaned down and said to him, "Don't ever do that, Josh. Daddy's got a lot on his mind tonight." Josh bit his lower lip and muttered okay. He quietly went off to his room.

Marla was on the phone in their bedroom. Bob had time to change, grab a quick bite, and take off for church, where his group met. He silently signaled for her to end her phone conversation and began to change clothes. "I've got evangelism tonight," he said after she had hung up.

"But I thought you were going to help Bev study for her math test tomorrow, and when are we going to go over the bills?" she asked in a voice dripping with disappointment. "We're getting behind, you know."

"Well, I'm sorry. You'll have to help Bev tonight," Bob

said, not trying to hide his impatience, "and can't the bills wait until tomorrow?" Bob loved his wife, but felt sometimes that she lacked spiritual vision. "Really, Mar, don't you think saving souls is more important than multiplication tables or paying some old bills? Is dinner ready yet?"

From the moment he pulled out of his driveway, Bob was overcome by feelings of guilt. He had a moment to reflect on the day's events and was consumed with guilt for not making the most of his available time. He felt like a failure in each of the important areas of his life: God, family, and his work. It was as if he spent all of his time running from fire to fire, trying to put it out until being called away by yet another fire.

And then suddenly Bob became angry. He felt like he'd been robbed. Violated. Eaten alive by the countless everyday events, circumstances, and occurrences that stole his time and kept him from doing the things he really wanted to do. He finished saying a quick prayer as he pulled into his church's parking lot 20 minutes late.

React and Respond

1. How do you respond when various areas of your life (e.g., work and family, or church and work, or leisure and family) conflict with each other?

2. When Jesus explained His parable of the sower, He described the meaning of the seed that falls upon thorns which eventually choke the life out of the plant: "The seed that fell among thorns stands for those who hear, but as they go on their way they are choked by life's worries, riches and pleasures, and they do not mature" (Luke 8:14). Jesus desires us always to keep our focus on Him. He promises to help us through the tough times—through the out-of-time, and at-the-end-of-my-rope times. Jesus invites us to give our problems and burdens over to Him and He promises to help us keep from getting choked out by the demands and pressures of life. Explain the promise contained in the following passage for someone caught in the great balancing act of effective time

management. "I love the LORD, for He heard my voice; He heard my cry for mercy. Because He turned His ear to me, I will call on Him as long as I live" (Psalm 116:1–2).

3. Reflect for a moment on the faithfulness of God in your life. Is there some problem in your life that you haven't given over to Him for His help? Why not? Why not talk to Him about it right now?

It's about Time

To a person anticipating a long-awaited event, time is an enemy. Plodding along slowly time shows no awareness of or concern for the person waiting no matter how impatient or anxious that person may become. To a person who sells his time—a lawyer, a doctor, an advertising executive—time is a comfortable friend—a billable commodity, broken down into quarter hours, and depending on the task performed, having a specific dollar value ascribed to it.

And yet to a person diagnosed with an incurable, fatal disease, time becomes more precious than gold—both a cruel enemy and the closest of allies. A recent headline in an ad for an international airline company read, "Time is everything." Does it follow that the ever-increasing number of men who find they have no time are anything?

A recent Wall Street Journal/NBC News survey of 2,001 people revealed that 59% describe their lives as busy and another 19% say their life has become busy to the point of discomfort. The real irony of the modern time crunch is that to conduct this survey, researchers had to dial 31,407 to find the 2,001 who actually had the time to answer the survey questions.

Time has become an endangered quantity in the modern world. Because we live in the instantaneous response and

21

option-centered frenzy provided by computers, faxes, microwaves, drive-throughs, cable TV, and the Internet, we now have more choices in work and leisure than ever before. These choices make greater demands on our time.

Communications technology makes us more accessible than ever before. People can reach us by phone (regular and cellular), fax, modem, or e-mail 24 hours a day. The question becomes when—or if—they dare turn these devices off. With increased accessibility comes less discretionary time of our own.

We must know more and be aware of more information than ever before. To compensate, we sometimes become quite adept at doing more than one thing at a time. We ride an exercycle while reading the day's newspaper while watching a documentary on TV. We listen to work tapes in our cars as we drive—and while listening and driving, we stop at drive-throughs to get something quick to eat.

As time slowly slips through the fingers of today's modern man, he is forced to realize the lack of control he has. He is powerless over the daily demands and choices that overwhelm and crowd him. Like the consumption of Eden's forbidden fruit, the technology and choices that promised to enlighten and liberate us have oppressed and enslaved us instead.

React and Respond

1. When we are knee deep in our lives and our faith is choked by the worries and concerns of this life, we can take comfort that God can break through the confusion and noise that distracts us and causes us to take our eyes off of the Lord. Our Lord Himself comforts and directs us, "Be still, and know that I am God; I will be exalted among the nations, I will be exalted in the earth" (Psalm 46:10). The Hebrew in this passage for "be still" is probably an expletive meaning "Enough!" Share a time when you were preoccupied with or worried about a situation and God broke through to comfort you and tell you, "Enough of worry and concern, know that I am God and will provide for you."

2. The pleasures and conveniences of this world are gifts to us from the hand of our loving and gracious God. Yet, we are not to put any of them before God. Neither are we to become too attached to them. John writes, "Do not love the world or anything of the world. If anyone loves the world, the love of the Father is not in him. For everything in the world—the cravings of sinful man, the lust of his eyes and the boasting of what he has and does—comes not from the Father but from the world. The world and its desires pass away, but the man who does the will of God lives forever" (1 John 2:15–17).

List three things you are very fond of. How could these items strain your relationship with God?

3. Later John writes, "This is love for God: to obey His commands. And His commands are not burdensome, for everyone born of God overcomes the world. This is the victory that has overcome the world, even our faith. Who is it that overcomes the world? Only He who believes that Jesus is the Son of God (1 John 5:3–5).

a. Knowing that Jesus' victory over sin, death, and the devil at Calvary's cross has earned forgiveness for all our sins, how does the promise of 1 John 5:3–5 make you feel?

b. Look back at your list from the last question; what does this promise mean to you, even if you can't eliminate or replace the worldly desires you listed with desires and motivations to obey and serve God?

c. Consider again the items on your list. How might the Holy Spirit lead and empower you to use these items to the glory of God?

23

God's Time, Not Ours

The way we live our lives can be compared to a man whose car is stalled on railroad tracks. Unable to move the car, the man is forced to wait, listening for the distant whistle to give him an indication of an approaching train. The train could come at any minute. Or, it could come much later. The only certainty about the situation is that eventually, a train will come.

The finality of life on this earth is certain. Think about it for a minute. In between this very moment and the time at which Jesus comes to take you to eternity is a set, fixed amount of time. Even though you don't know how much time you'll be given, you know it's a finite amount. God determines how much time each of us have. The psalmist writes, "But I trust in You, O LORD: I say, 'You are my God. My times are in Your hands'" (Psalm 31:15). Whether we find ourselves in the eastern, central, mountain, or pacific time zones, we are still living in God's time zone.

Time is a precious gift given to each of us by God. And God has a reason and purpose behind everything He allows to happen in the time He has given to us and throughout all of history. Because God's perfect patience and long-suffering nature, He gives all of us as much time as possible to repent and be saved. Plus, He has given those of us who belong to Him a plan and purpose which He would have us accomplish for Him in the time He has given us.

React and Respond

1. There are many parables in the Bible about people and how they spend their time.

a. Read Jesus' parable about the rich fool found in Luke 12:15–21. When have you felt like the rich fool?

b. How can people be "rich toward God" (v. 21)?

2. Read Matthew 12:1–8. Applying the message of these verses to your own life, what helpful distinction can God's people make between giving attention to the details of this life and the things of God?

3. When Jesus visited Martha's home, she complained to Jesus that her sister, Mary, was not helping with the preparations. Instead Mary was listening to Jesus' Words. Jesus responded to her, "Martha, Martha," the Lord answered, "you are worried and upset about many things, but only one thing is needed. Mary has chosen what is better, and it will not be taken away from her." What benefit do God's people derive when by the Spirit's power they receive God's Word in faith? (See 1 Thessalonians 2:13.)

The Inevitable Fruit

When by God's grace a person receives the saving faith in Jesus Christ, the Holy Spirit begins a work in the believer. Through a process called sanctification, God's Spirit works through the Word to conform the believer to the likeness of his Master. As a result, God's presence evidences itself in our lives and we inevitably bear fruit.

The apostle Paul, writing to the Colossians (1:9–12) says: "For this reason, since the day we heard about you, we have not stopped praying for you and asking God to fill you with the knowledge of His will through all spiritual wisdom and understanding. And we pray this in order that **you may live a life worthy of the Lord and may please Him in every way: bearing fruit in every good work** (emphasis added), growing in the knowledge of God, being strengthened with all power according to His glorious might so that you may have great endurance and patience, and joyfully giving thanks to the Father, who has qualified you to share in the inheritence of the saints in the kingdom of light."

When God graciously fills us with knowledge of His will through spiritual wisdom and understanding, His Spirit's power enables us to dedicate our lives to Him who died for us and rose again. The Holy Spirit works this same knowledge and grace in our hearts by providing a presence of godly attitudes, actions, and characteristics. As believers grow and mature, the Spirit causes these characteristics—called fruit of the Spirit—to result and to increase over time in their lives: love, joy, peace, patience, kindness, goodness, faithfulness, gentleness, and self-control (Galatians 5:22–23).

Make no mistake about it. There are no "10 easy steps" to increase these characteristics in your life. No 12-step program for improving your fruitfulness. You can't "will yourself" into having more self-control or love.

We are dependent completely upon God for fruitfulness. Only through His Word has God's Spirit promised to work faith and the results of a Spirit-directed life. We depend completely on God to bear the highly desirable good fruit in our lives. John records our Savior's words, "I am the vine; you are the branches. If a man remains in Me and I in him, he will bear much fruit; apart from Me you can do nothing. If anyone does not remain in Me, he is like a branch that is thrown away and withers; such branches are picked up, thrown into the fire and burned. If you remain in Me and My words remain in you, ask whatever you wish, and it will be given you. This is to My Father's glory, that you bear much fruit, showing yourselves to be My disciples" (John 15:5–8).

React and Respond

1. Writing by inspiration, Titus says that we are identified by the fruit we produce in every area of our lives, "For the grace of God that brings salvation has appeared to all men. It teaches us to say "No" to ungodliness and worldly passions, and to live self-controlled, upright and godly lives" (Titus 2:11–12).

Grace has been explained using the following acronym:

God's
Riches
At
Christ's
Expense

How has "the grace of God that brings salvation ... appeared to all men?"

2. What results occur in the lives of those who by faith receive God's gift of grace and allow it to transform their lives?

3. What evidence of the power of God's grace can you cite from your own life or the lives of other Christian men?

Guiding Principles

When managing our time and being a good steward of this precious resource granted to us in God's measure, there should be two guiding principles. In all that we do, we must always consider these two underlying foundations that will determine everything we do, and conversely, everything we don't.

By asking Jesus which of the commandments was the greatest, an expert in God's Law was once trying to entrap Jesus. We can assume Jesus' response was not what the teacher was expecting. Jesus replied, " 'Love the Lord your God with all your heart and with all your soul and with all your mind.' This is the first and greatest commandment" (Matthew 22:37–38).

As a result of one man's misguided attempt, a great truth was revealed to us about priorities. A truth that was there in the law all along, and Jesus clearly expressed and revealed it to us.

God comes first. He desires our love for Him to permeate every realm of our being. He wants us to seek Him, to worship Him, and to open our hearts and our lives and our thoughts to Him. Because we fall short of this, Christ went willingly to the cross to suffer and die for us. His power defeated sin and death for us. His same power increases the love we have for Him and the devotion we exhibit in our everyday actions.

And then, Jesus continued, "And the second is like it: 'Love your neighbor as yourself.' All the Law and the Prophets hang on these two commandments" (Matthew 22:39–40).

Who is our neighbor? Our enemies. Our friends. Our family and relatives. Our co-workers. Our bosses. Our staff that we manage. Our fellow churchgoers. The parameters for defining the term *neighbor* is a simple one—any human being alive on the planet earth is our neighbor.

Aren't these two rules amazing? Every single law contained in the Bible, *all* of them are encapsulated by these two simple thoughts: love God and love your neighbor. So simple, a child could understand them. Yet so lofty a standard that no sinner can ever fulfill them.

When the Spirit of God moved us to base all of our action and inaction upon these two principles, a prioritization of our tasks often falls into place. If the motivation for a potential action finds its origin in our love for God or our neighbors, we honor God in our doing of it. If a potential action is not founded in love, God's Spirit would have us avoid it.

God has a structure for the love we have in our lives. The hierarchy of love is as follows:

God

Family

Work

Everything in the family and work spheres is a subset of the God sphere. For instance, when we raise a God-fearing family in an environment of love, acceptance, and forgiveness, we are serving God. Everything we do for our family—serve, lead, protect, provide for, nurture, encourage, and love—we are doing for the glory of God.

Similarly, we can also serve God by everything we do in our work and occupations. In attitudes and actions that are good, loyal, hardworking, trustworthy, dependable, cheerful, and resourceful, and loving to workers and co-workers, we glorify God as His Spirit works in us through the Word of God.

Taking Jesus with you into every aspect of your life and into every situation you encounter during the day will help keep you from becoming distracted with one thing or another. In starting each day, take a few minutes to map out a course of action. What things can you do to glorify God? What things can you do for your neighbors to express love? Think of it a couple of times during the day to help you to stay on the course.

God's Spirit helps sensitize us for opportunities to serve God during the course of each day in special, unique, and often exciting and unlikely and unpredictable ways. We will still fall short in our desire to serve God faithfully in our thoughts, words, and actions. But God's forgiveness and strength are always there for us. Jesus earned them, paying the ultimate cost, and they will never be taken away from us.

One day Jesus will take us to live with Him in heaven, where we will experience perfect happiness in an existence unconcerned about time. Meanwhile we remain God's men—men with a mission.

React and Respond

1. A popular Christian motto carries the sentiment,

> Only one life will soon be past.
> Only what's done for Christ will last.

Explain these words and any application they may have for your life.

2. Concerned about his life and priorities, a young man once went to his father, a dedicated Christian, for some sound advice about how to organize and live his life to the glory of God. The father's response came in the form of two simple words, "Be balanced!" Do you agree with the father's advice? Why or why not?

3 How Well Do You Do Your Living?

"Dyin' ain't important. Everybody does that. What matters is how well you do your livin'."

A Matter of Integrity

"We're going to do something a little bit different today," the teacher announced. "We're going to play a game."

A game? Jerry thought to himself. His body language conveyed his feelings about the whole idea, how stupid. What are we supposed to learn from a dumb game? He squirmed in his desk.

"Ms. Forte will hand out envelopes to each of you," Mr. Clawson, one of Jerry's two teachers continued. "Don't open them up until I tell you."

Mr. Clawson neatly wrote the name of each student on the blackboard. When he had finished, he turned around and waited for Ms. Forte to hand out the last of the envelopes. "Jeremy Abrams. Open your envelope, please." He waited as Jerry opened his envelope. "What do you have there?"

"A bunch of different colored pieces of paper," Jerry answered, studying and counting the blank slips of paper.

"How many gold do you have?" Mr. Clawson asked, his piece of chalk poised, hovering over a point next to Jerry's name.

"Five." Mr. Clawson recorded it on the blackboard. "And how many black?" "Three." "Red?" "Seven." "Blue?" "Five." After he had finished writing down the tallies for each color, he turned to the next student and did the same.

When he had finished tallying everyone's colored slips, the teacher addressed the whole class, "Today, you're all going to be companies. The colored slips of paper you have represent commerce. Money. The different colors represent different denominations of the currency. One gold equals five blacks. One black equals three reds. One red equals two blues."

Suddenly the eyes of every student were peeled to the board. The money hadn't been distributed equally. A few of

30

the students had a lot of golds and blacks. Some had no golds and few blacks. Most of the students had a few of each color. The mix of shouts of glee and moans of disappointment filled the classroom.

"There will be four-minute trading periods when you can exchange money with whomever you wish. The only rule is that in order for a trade to take place, both parties have to agree."

"That's it?" Jerry asked his friend, Philip, next to him, "This oughta be easy. Wanna be partners? Mr. Clawson didn't say anything about not being able to form teams."

"Okay," Philip answered.

Mr. Clawson continued, "Ms. Forte will be the bank. She can make loans to you for trading sessions, but you have to pay her back with interest after the trading session is over. She can make change for you and will pay you one red ticket per trading period for each gold ticket you keep locked up in her bank." Ms. Forte waived meekly. A large transparent garbage bag was next to her. It was filled with different colored tickets.

Mr. Clawson looked at his watch. "Everyone ... begin trading. You have four minutes."

With one last glance at the big bag of money, Jerry turned to Philip, "You go work on Jack Stevens. I'm going to try to see what I can do with Matt Zurich. They're both pretty weak. We ought to be able to come out ahead with those guys." The first trading session was rather uneventful; the students awkwardly talked and exchanged money until Mr Clawson interrupted. "Stop trading. Lets count the tickets."

Jerry stared at his own tickets. Philip came up to him. Between the two of them, they had roughly about the same amount of money as when they started. The next trading session was the same. As was the one after that.

Jerry realized that unless he did something different, Philip and he wouldn't be very successful. He went over to Philip.

"Phil, you go over and get Jim and Steve. They didn't get many good tickets, and they don't look like they care about this game anyway. Get them to join us. We'll put all our money together and win! I'm going to go over here and see what I can do." Philip went off in search of Jim and Steve.

Jerry went over to the desk directly behind the table on which Ms. Forte was lending and borrowing colored tickets. When he felt sure Ms. Forte wasn't paying close attention, Jerry stuck his hand into the bag and pulled out a fistful of colored slips. He quickly stuffed them in his pocket. Then he repeated the procedure a couple of times.

Jerry briefly felt sorry for Ms. Forte, but quickly reasoned that it was just a game. The paper was only paper, anyway. It wasn't like it was real money. And after all, the game only had one rule.

After Mr. Clawson had signaled the end of another trading period, Philip, Jim, Steve, and Jerry huddled together to count their loot in the center of the room. The fruits of their labors were evident in the uncounted stack of colored slips.

They started to gloat. "Amy Graham is so stupid. She traded me seven blacks for one gold!" "I know, Jeff gave me all his gold because I told him to! What a wus!"

Each of the other boys was sharing his individual conquest, when Jerry got in the middle of them and said quietly, "Yeah? Well look at this." He pulled out the wad of money from his pockets. Each of the boys moved in close around Jerry to make sure no one else saw. They could scarcely contain their happiness and excitement.

Ms. Forte interrupted their celebration with an announcement. "Okay, you remember there was only one rule regarding the trading? Now we're going to do things a little bit differently. From now on, the company or conglomeration with the most tickets after each trading period is allowed to make up three rules—anything the company wants."

Philip, Jerry, Steve, and Jim had more than twice as many ticket as any person or team. They got together and began to discuss what their three new rules would be. Their heads were swimming with the possibilities. This new twist to the game intoxicated the four boys.

The first rules the boys designed humiliated those with whom they traded. The four boys giggled and snickered as they read their three new rules aloud to the class.

One rule required others to make trades with the four of them while on their knees. Another rule made others kiss their hands before they asked permission to trade. The final rule required everyone to initiate any trade with the words, "I, sir, am a wiggly worm, sir, from the depths of the earth, sir. Won't you please consider making a trade with me, sir?"

The scene of mass humiliation was almost more excitement and thrill than Philip, Jerry, Steve, and Jim could handle. It was a hurricane of fun; they were in the eye of the storm and they loved it.

Through the years, Jerry hadn't thought that much about the game his class had played way back in elementary school. But today, for some reason, the memory surfaced. Jerry was in the middle of a difficult time at work. It was the night before a big presentation and he'd noticed a problem with one of the designs Rick was proposing. Rick, a co-worker, happened to be in the running with Jerry for an upcoming promotion.

Over the past few months, things had gotten a little ugly between the two of them. Now Jerry toyed with the idea of not telling Rick about the problem he'd found with his design. He imagined what it would be like to watch Rick slit his professional wrists right in front of the managing partners of the firm and the firm's most important client.

In the midst of his current, personal turmoil, Jerry paused for a moment to think back to that day so long ago. Smiling, He remembered the fun he had had—the thrill, the excitement—when a strange thought occurred to him. Wouldn't it have been obvious to Ms. Forte why he had taken a seat directly behind her? Wouldn't she have known he was up to something when he sat out an entire trading period? At the very least, she must have thought it odd. The more he thought about it, the less he was sure she was oblivious to his thievery.

And then another thought occurred to him. Even though the afternoon's activity appeared on the surface to be chaotic and loosey-goosey, with little or no rules or guidelines, the game had only one outcome. If Philip, Jerry, Steve, and Jim hadn't risen to the top of things, some other team or person would have. That was the whole idea of the game—to expose the dark, ugly, succeed-at-all-costs side of people. The teachers knew all along what would happen.

Suddenly Jerry felt like he had been identified with the underside of humanity. In the past. And right now. He felt sorry, ashamed, and worthless for something that happened so many years ago. He felt worse about what he had contemplated doing to Rick.

REACT AND RESPONd

1. Think about a time when you felt like Jerry. React to each of the following passages as you reflect upon this particular event or situation.

a. "Surely I was sinful at birth, sinful from the time my mother conceived me" (a reflection of David recorded in Psalm 51:5).

b. "Godly sorrow brings repentance that leads to salvation and leaves no regret, but worldly sorrow brings death" (2 Corinthians 7:10).

c. "God made Him [Jesus] who had no sin to be sin for us, so that in Him we might become the righteousness of God" (2 Corinthians 5:21).

2. Researchers studing habits in the American workplace report an alarmingly high number of people willing to commit fraud. "We all know 'honesty is the best policy.' Nobody has to teach us that." Explain this statement in light of the following verses.

a. "Indeed, when Gentiles, who do not have the law, do by nature things required by the law, they are a law for themselves, even though they do not have the law, since they show that the requirements of the law are written on their hearts, their consciences also bearing witness, and their thoughts now accusing, now even defending them" (Romans 2:14–15).

b. "Do not have two differing weights in your bag—one heavy, one light. Do not have two differing measures in your house—one large, one small. You must have accurate and honest weights and measures, so that you may live long in the land the LORD your God is giving you. For the LORD your God detests anyone who does these things, anyone who deals dishonestly" (Deuteronomy 25:13–16).

c. "Honest scales and balances are from the LORD; all the weights in the bag are of His making" (Proverbs 16:11).

3. Jesus is the only truly honest man who ever lived. He dealt with all others with perfect honesty and integrity in our place and, also in our place, died to pay the penalty our sins deserved. Once He comes into a human life, that person is never the same again.

a. Zacchaeus made his living as a chief tax collector. As such, he held a position notorious for corruption and unsavory dealings. When Jesus entered his life, Zacchaeus responded, "Look, Lord! Here and now I give half of my possessions to the poor, and if I have cheated anybody out of anything, I will pay back four times the amount" (Luke 19:8). Explain Zacchaeus' response.

b. With the forgiveness brought to us by Jesus, our Savior and friend, comes new desires and goals. 2 Corinthians 5:17 records, "Therefore, if anyone is in Christ, he is a new creation; the old has gone, the new has come!" Give examples of this Christ-brought newness in your life or in the lives of those you know.

Jungle Warfare

As we go about our routines at work, it's easy to forget there is more to our daily agenda than meets the eye. Each of God's people faces a spiritual battlefield each day. When we walk into the office of a male friend and begin talking about the new woman on the floor in an inappropriate way, when we become angry and envious over a co-worker's bonus, when we sink another's reputation with inappropriate comments or gossip—in these times—as in all others—we experience a struggle between the dead weight of our sinful nature pulling us down and the higher promptings of the Holy Spirit working in us the desire and power to walk in Christ's light.

When we compromise ourselves and act or continue to act in sin, we give victory to Satan. Even though he has been judged and his future is certain, he wants to take as many souls with him as he can and he constantly looks for ways to defeat God's divine plans of grace. Sometimes we fail. We sin against God and turn our backs on Him. Satan's desire is for God's people to feel comfortable dominated by sin so that we shut God out of our lives entirely.

But despite our sinful inclinations, God delights in people—the pinnacle of His creation. God loved us so much that He sent His only-begotten Son to die for us and redeem us from sin. Because of what Christ has done for us, God invites and empowers us to turn and return to God when we fail, just as the wayward, prodigal son returned to his father in sorrow, shame, and humility but confident nonetheless of His fathers unending and unconditional loving acceptance. When we confess our sins, God who is faithful forgives us our sins for the sake of His Son. And when we repent, there is much rejoicing. It's as if God runs out to greet us and celebrates with us over our return to His fold.

React and Respond

1. Who would have known better the subtleties of deadly spiritual warfare than the apostle Peter. Peter, you'll recall, couldn't keep awake during his Lord's agony in Gethsemane and later betrayed his Lord out of fear for his physical well-being. In 1 Peter 5:8, he reassures us that our struggles are not unique to us:

> Be self-controlled and alert. Your enemy the devil prowls around like a roaring lion looking for someone to devour. Resist him, standing firm in the faith, because you know that your brothers throughout the world are undergoing the same kind of sufferings.

a. What evidence of the lion's prowling do you find in your life?

b. What can we do to help our brothers "throughout the world" who are undergoing the same kind of sufferings?

2. It's a jungle out there and daily we struggle to live lives of honesty and integrity. God knows this. God knows us.

> As a father has compassion on his children, so the LORD has compassion on those who fear Him; for He knows how we are formed, He remembers that we are dust. (Psalm 103:13–14)

How does God, who knows us better than we know ourselves, help us in our spiritual battles according to each of the following passages?

a. "Put on the full armor of God so that you can take your stand against the devil's schemes. Take the helmet of salvation and the sword of the Spirit, which is the Word of God" (Ephesians 6:11, 17).

b. "[Jesus said,] 'Come to Me, all you who are weary and burdened, and I will give you rest. Take My yoke upon you and learn from Me, for I am gentle and humble in heart, and you will find rest for your souls' " (Matthew 11:28–29).

c. "He who began a good work in you will carry it on to completion until the day of Christ Jesus" (Philippians 1:6).

d. "Consider it pure joy, my brothers, whenever you face trials of many kinds, because you know that the testing of your faith develops perseverance" (James 1:2–3).

An Example of Integrity

Where then can an honest man be found? God has recorded an excellent example of an honest man for us to study in the book of Genesis.

Joseph was sold into slavery by his brothers. The Ishmaelites who bought Joseph took him to Egypt where he was sold a second time to Potiphar, an Egyptian who was one of Pharaoh's officials, the captain of the guard. Throughout the story, there is not one instance that even suggests Joseph grumbled or complained about the unfortunate turn of events so suddenly and unjustly thrust upon him. Instead God's Word records, "The LORD was with Joseph and he prospered" (Genesis 39:2).

The next verses, Genesis 39:3–4, point out an important point for God's people to remember. "When his master saw that the LORD was with him and that the LORD gave him success in everything he did, Joseph found favor in his eyes and became his attendant. Potiphar put him in charge of his household, and he entrusted to his care everything he owned."

When we heed the quiet urgings and promptings of the Holy Spirit rather than the loud, consistent screaming of the world, one of two things usually happens: We draw attention to ourselves, and secondly and of greater importance, we draw attention to God. Potiphar attributed Joseph's success to the presence of God in his life. Potiphar most likely came to realize the true God's power and presence in Joseph's life because Joseph credited God for His successes.

Next Joseph is forced to contend with the temptation to sin against God in his workplace. "Now Joseph was well-built and handsome, and after a while his master's wife took notice of Joseph and said, 'Come to bed with me!' " (Genesis 38:6–7).

Joseph takes two things into consideration when confronted with this temptation to commit adultery. First, he considers the trust placed in him by his master, Potiphar. Even though Joseph was a stranger in a strange land, sold into slavery, through no fault of his own and forced to work for Potiphar, Joseph would not cross him by committing adultery with his wife. His first thought when tempted to commit sin was not satisfaction of his primal instincts, but betraying the trust of his master. Second, Joseph recognizes the proposition for what it is: a wicked act of sin against God. Through the working of God's Spirit, Joseph recognized immediately the results this sin would have on his relationship with God. He did not try to justify or rationalize the act. Instead He relied on the strength God provided and refused to give in to the opportunity to sin.

Verse 10 records, "And though she spoke to Joseph day after day, he refused to go to bed with her or even be with her." Note that Joseph does not waiver in his conviction that this act is wrong. He consistently turns away from this sin though Potiphar's wife tempted him "day after day." Further, it seems Joseph formulated a plan for staying clear of sin; he "refused ... to even be with her."

Finally, Joseph is accused of committing the very act which he was so successful in avoiding. Believing his wife's false accusations, Potiphar becomes furious with Joseph and has him thrown into prison. But even prison could not isolate Joseph from God's guiding and success-giving love and care.

React and Respond

1. Joseph's master took notice of his work. But what about when men of God do good things at work and no one notices? Consider Colossians 3:23–24 as part of your response.

> Whatever you do, work at it with all your heart, as working for the Lord, not for men, since you know that you will receive an inheritance from the Lord as a reward. It is the Lord Christ you are serving.

2. Reflect on the following passage together with the example of Joseph as you formulate a plan for dealing with temptations that occur in the workplace.

> No temptation has seized you except what is common to man. And God is faithful; He will not let you be tempted beyond what you can bear. But when you are tempted, He will also provide a way out so that you can stand up under it. (1 Corinthians 10:13)

3. What unique opportunities do each of the following provide for giving glory and honor to God?

a. You experience a setback at work.

b. You receive praise or accolades for something you accomplished.

c. You make the major contribution to a successful project for which everyone involved receives equal credit.

Forward into Battle

Over time, as the Spirit of God changes us through God's Word, an awesome thing takes place; we begin to identify more and more with God and the Holy Spirit and less and less with our sinful desires and propensities. By enabling us to yield to the direction and empowerment of the Holy Spirit, God's power works to diminish the stranglehold sin has over us in our lives.

We may never know how God uses a demonstration of integrity, a selfless act of kindness, or a willingness to advance another at our own expense to open the door for the Gospel. We grow close to those with whom we work; we can't help it. Working with others means by necessity sharing personal and professional joys and sorrows. Opportunities will arise to tell someone the Good News of Jesus. Consider the experience of Rob.

Rob was at work when he got the call about Jim. Jim was absent from work that day; he had called in sick. But Jim wasn't sick. Not physically at least. Jim stayed home that day and he was alone. Jim was alone because his wife had left him for another. Despondent, Jim had attempted to take his life. Having failed in his attempt, he had been admitted into a local hospital. Rob was requested to visit Jim after work.

Jim's first question, "How do you get through the tough times in your life, Rob? I know you're a Christian. But what does it mean to be a Christian, really?"

Rob had been waiting and praying for an opportunity to talk to Jim about Jesus. Now here was Jim, practically pleading for the Good News of Jesus. Rob was eager and prepared to acquaint Jim with His best friend and Savior.

Battles provide opportunities to evidence courage and to glorify God. By glorifying God in our thoughts, words, and deeds we accomplish something amazing on another level:

> You are the light of the world. A city on a hill cannot be hidden. Neither do people light a lamp and put it under a bowl. Instead they put it on its stand, and it gives light to everyone in the house. In the same way, let your light shine before men, that they may see your good deeds and praise your Father in heaven. (Matthew 5:14–16)

There will be times when we stumble. But through Christ's death and resurrection, we've already won the war.

React and Respond

1. Why may Jim have turned to Rob for answers during his time of need? Share about a time when, like Rob, God gave you an opportunity to tell a co-worker about Jesus.

2. Mark was known at work for his intimate details about the shortcomings of others and his ability to originate humor at the expense of co-workers. After becoming a Christian, Mark focused on a goal of changing his communication habits. Why do you think Mark choose this goal for himself?

3. What goal could you adopt to help your light shine more brightly at work?

4 A Good and Faithful Worker

A Struggle with Obedience

It was 1969. A summer of love for some young men. A summer of war for others.

Tony awaited a trip to a hospital in Da Nang. He had been coughing up blood the last couple of weeks. The doctors said that the change in climate was wreaking havoc with his twenty-one-year-old lungs. The midwestern humidity paled in comparison to the muggy days and nights in the thick, dripping jungles of Vietnam.

A well-trained soldier, Tony was used to obeying without question. Doing what he was told kept him alive. Some days it was all that kept him going.

Tony was being transported by a Medvac medical chopper. The big, red cross on the chopper's side reassured Tony that he and the other occupants of the craft would be safe. They were not likely to be shot at by the enemy.

After Tony climbed aboard, the chopper rose into the air and a loud staticy noise pierced the steady drone of the aircraft's blades. It was the radio. The pilot was ordered to stop and pick up some wounded from a firefight somewhere below them on the ground. Reluctantly, the pilot radioed an acknowledgment of his orders and proceeded to point the helicopter toward the coordinates of the skirmish.

Tony started to get nervous as the chopper approached the ground. The American soldiers were still in the middle of the fight. He heard the noises he had learned to hate—yelling, screaming, pain, fear, confusion, death; these were the noises of war and they made him shudder.

The Medvac touched down and the pilot quickly hopped out keeping his head down so far, Tony wondered how he could possible see where he was going. The bullets whizzed by closely; Tony imagined he could see them. Like black shadows, the sounds randomly darted about. Tony began searching for his M-16. If something happened to the pilot, Tony would be on his own for survival. He had to be ready for that possibility.

Finally the pilot returned and two wounded men were loaded onto the chopper. The first was an unconscious American. He was put in the rear of the Medvac. The second was a Vietnamese prisoner.

"Keep an eye on this guy," the pilot told Tony as he threw the body of the bleeding man into Tony's arms, "and don't let him try any funny stuff." When Tony had first climbed aboard, he had noticed the pilot's fatigues. Lieutenant insignias neatly sewn on the pilot's clothing identified him as Tony's superior.

Red, Vietnamese blood mixed with Tony's dark green GI shirt turning it a rich black, shiny color as the writhing prisoner rattled on in panicky Vietnamese. Blood dripped all over the Vietcong's face as he moved his head from side to side, desperate to communicate pleas ... or something. Tony's first concern wasn't what the Vietcong was trying to say to him, or his physical comfort or lack thereof. His very first thought was checking this guy to make sure he didn't have any hidden weapons. He watched carefully to make sure the prisoner didn't make any sudden moves, like reaching for an unseen grenade or a homemade knife.

Tony suddenly began to feel sorry for this prisoner. He knew what was in store for him. The whole reason they were even bothering with this Vietcong soldier was for the information he might be able to provide. If American lives could be saved through something the Vietcong would reveal, patching up and caring for him would be worth the effort.

Even though Tony was sympathetic in a distant way, he still kept a close eye and a tight grip on the prisoner. No sudden moves. Tony would do whatever it took to stay alive. Staying alive is after all what wartime soldiering is all about.

The pilot took off quickly and got away from the skirmish. Tony glanced down at his watch. Seven minutes? Were they really there for less than 10 minutes? It had seemed like a good half hour or longer to Tony.

Tony and the rest were cruising along about 500 feet above the ground. Then the pilot took off his sunglasses and turned around to Tony, who was right behind him. His hazel green eyes narrowed in a menacing squint.

"Push the prisoner out!" The pilot commanded. His hands never left the helicopter's controls as he waited for Tony to comply.

Tony took his gaze off the prisoner for a moment and searched the lieutenant's face. Had he really heard what he just thought he had heard? Maybe this man was joking with him.

"What?" Tony asked, afraid of what the answer was going to be.

"Push him out! Now! Do it!"

War, Tony suddenly thought, is funny. This lieutenant commander was ordered to pick up some wounded, one of whom was a Vietnamese prisoner. And now this same commander had turned and ordered him to toss the fully conscious man out the door to a 500 foot drop and a certain, gruesome death. It didn't make sense.

Tony was sinking in the dilemma: He didn't think he could carry the order out, yet if he didn't, he would be disobeying a superior officer. Tony began to think of the potential consequences of disobedience. Disobeying was a very serious offense. He could be courtmartialed. He could face a long jail sentence. But he couldn't kill another innocent human being, even this pathetic, little, wounded stranger.

"I ... I ... I just don't think I can do that, Lieutenant ...," Tony managed to stammer.

Tony was shocked at what was happening. Death was all around him. He could smell it. One stray bullet or piece of flying shrapnel and his life would be over. And now he had this to worry about.

"C'mon. Just do it and we'll tell them the guy died and we had to get rid of the body," the lieutenant urged him. "They'll believe it. They won't think twice about it."

Tony thought about how easy it would be to just give this frightened, quivering human being a shove and this situation would be over. No one would know about it. This pilot wouldn't tell anyone the truth. Tony suddenly stiffened.

"He's not going anywhere," Tony said, his voice suddenly getting stronger. Tony didn't even realize he was pulling the prisoner closer to himself, locking his arms around the man.

The lieutenant's face turned red. He began to scream as large bits of saliva were launched from his mouth.

"I know who you are now! I've got your name! Your name's going to be s#$%!"

If word got out that Tony had saved the life of an enemy, it could be a serious problem. There were a lot of soldiers who were ruthless in carrying out their job of killing as many enemy as they could. Tony would run the risk of being confronted by one of them. And if he did, well, Tony began to sweat as he thought about that possibility. "What are you, one of the enemy?" would be the question they would most certainly ask him.

And then it hit Tony right between the eyes: This lieutenant was, himself, one of those ruthless soldiers with a strong love for killing the enemy. The pilot turned back to his controls, cursing madly under his breath. Tony's dilemma was over. He should have felt relieved. Instead he just felt numb.

The prisoner was still jabbering on in Vietnamese. This man had no idea how close he had just come to being killed. Tony began to sob into his shoulder.

But no tears came out.

React and Respond

1. God desires us to obey those He has placed in positions of authority over us. At the same time, He would also have us honor Him with respect to all of His other commandments. Because we live in a sin-contaminated world, we often face difficult choices between right and wrong. Sometimes we must even choose between wrong and more wrong. How would you have handled Tony's situation had you been in his place? Would Tony have been responsible for his actions against the prisoner since he was simply following the orders of an officer of a higher rank?

2. Have you ever found yourself in a situation where your boss or someone in authority over you asked you to do something you thought was wrong? How did you respond? What happened as a result of your response?

3. Acts 4–5 tell of a time when Peter and John faced a dilemma similar to Tony's. What choice did Peter and John face? Why do you think they responded as they did?

> Then they called them in again and commanded them not to speak or teach at all in the name of Jesus. But Peter and John replied, "Judge for yourselves whether it is right in God's sight to obey you rather than God. For we cannot help speaking about what we have seen and heard." (Acts 4:18–19)
>
> Having brought the apostles, they made them appear before the Sanhedrin to be questioned by the high priest. "We gave you strict orders not to teach in this name," he said. "Yet you have filled Jerusalem with your teaching and are determined to make us guilty of this man's blood." Peter and the other apostles replied: "We must obey God rather than men! The God of our fathers raised Jesus from the dead—whom you had killed by hanging Him on a tree. God exalted Him to His own right hand as Prince and Savior that He might give repentance and forgiveness of sins to Israel. We are witnesses of these things, and so is the Holy Spirit, whom God has given to those who obey Him." (Acts 5:27–32)

4. Acts 1:8 records Jesus' words of commission to His disciples before He ascended into heaven, "But you will receive power when the Holy Spirit comes on you; and you will be My witnesses in Jerusalem, and in all Judea and Samaria, and to the ends of the earth."

a. How does the primary objective of God's people help

Christians to decide on an appropriate course of action when faced with opposition to God and His will?

b. What issues affect the witness we present to other fellow believers and to the unbelievers around us?

Service

It used to be that the only way to buy gasoline was from a full-service dealer. You'd pull in, request the familiar, "Fill 'er up," and then you could sit back and wait while the attendant not only filled up your gas tank, but also checked your oil, checked the air pressure in all of your tires (including your spare), and cleaned all your windows.

Today, full-service gas stations are all but extinct. Drivers want self-serve. We want to pay less and do everything ourselves. We may wonder: has serving others gone out of style?

React and Respond

1. A family movie told the story of a very wealthy, elderly woman who suddenly lost all of her money. The loyal employees who worked for her didn't want the woman to know what had happened to her, so they raised and sold vegetables in order to support the woman in the manner to which she had long been accustomed. "Can you imagine employees so loyal to their employer?" the husband asked his wife after the children went to bed.

"My grandmother was that kind of employee," responded his wife.

What do you think—do examples of extreme loyalty to the company or employer still exist in our world today, or has serving others gone out of style? Explain your response.

47

2. Consider the Word of God on the subject of serving those in authority over us:

"Everyone must submit himself to the governing authorities, for there is no authority except that which God has established. The authorities that exist have been established by God. Consequently, he who rebels against the authority is rebelling against what God has instituted, and those who do so will bring judgment on themselves. For rulers hold no terror for those who do right, but for those who do wrong. Do you want to be free from fear of the one in authority? Then do what is right and he will commend you. For he is God's servant to do you good. But if you do wrong, be afraid, for he does not bear the sword for nothing. He is God's servant, an agent of wrath to bring punishment on the wrongdoer. Therefore, it is necessary to submit to the authorities, not only because of possible punishment but also because of conscience." (Romans 13:1–5)

a. Who has established the authorities in our lives?

b. Verse 4 indicates that authorities are God's servants to do us good. Think about those you report to at work. What gifts does God give you, either directly or indirectly, through them?

c. As Jesus our Savior has lived and died for us, the Holy Spirit moves in us the desire to live our lives for God. Verse 5 speaks of submitting to authorities as a matter of conscience. According to the following verse in which Paul talks about himself, how can our conscience assist us in living the Christian life professionally and in every other aspect of our lives?

Now this is our boast: Our conscience testifies that we have conducted ourselves in the world, and especially in our relations with you, in the holiness and sincerity that are from God. We have done so not according to worldly wisdom but according to God's grace. (2 Corinthians 1:12)

In a Dog-Eat-Dog World

When two dogs engage in a confrontation with each other, they will fight it out, but sooner or later, one of the dogs will suddenly become submissive to the other. One of the dogs will roll over on his back, exposing his neck and jugular vein to the other dog. This is an act that says, "I am less than you are. I am weaker. You have authority over me. Do with me as you will."

Our natural instincts tell us that submission evidences weakness and resignation. We want to avoid appearing weak and helpless at all costs because we have been taught that weakness makes a male less of a man. Could it be that each of the following male stereotypes find their origin in an attempt to keep from appearing weak and incapable?

- an unwillingness to admit to being wrong
- a reluctance to stop and ask for directions when obviously lost
- a desire to exercise authority, particularly over wives and children
- a resistance to being open and vulnerable even to those closest to us
- a general attitude of I'll do it myself

Jesus has shown us excellent manhood. Leaving His heavenly throne, the maker and redeemer of the entire universe came to give rather than to receive.

To earn our forgiveness, a new beginning, and a forever-home in heaven, Jesus came to earth to serve us. He lived the perfect life we could not live and died a horrible death to pay the penalty our sins deserved. His resurrection assures us of His mastery over sin, death, and the devil. Yet Jesus did all of this in service to us because He loves us. Today Jesus remains our servant. Promising always to remain with us by the power of His Holy Spirit He continues to grow and nur-

49

ture us into the men of God He would have us become as He changes us through His Word.

Speaking to His disciples, Jesus said, "You know that the rulers of the Gentiles lord it over them, and their high officials exercise authority over them. Not so with you. Instead, whoever wants to become great among you must be your servant, and whoever wants to be first must be your slave—just as the Son of Man did not come to be served, but to serve, and to give His life as a ransom for many" (Matthew 20:25–28).

React and Respond

1. In 1 Corinthians 1:27 Paul records, "God chose the foolish things of the world to shame the wise; God chose the weak things of the world to shame the strong." Later, to the same group of believers Paul wrote these words of Jesus, "My grace is sufficient for you, for My power is made perfect in weakness." Paul says he would be glad about his weaknesses, hardships, and persecutions because when he was weak, Christ's power strengthened him (2 Corinthians 12:9–10). How do Paul's Words define our relationship with Christ?

2. As the Holy Spirit continues to work in your life as a man of God, what changes will result in your attitude toward each of the following:

a. your boss and others in authority over you

b. your co-workers

c. the clients and customers with whom you interact

3. Knowing that those in authority over us have been placed there by God Himself, we can also rest assured that God desires to claim their hearts for Himself, perhaps through the daily interaction they have with us. When God's people submit to those placed in authority over them as a witness to God's power within them, amazing things can happen. Apply the following account to the witness of any Christian man in the workplace.

About midnight Paul and Silas were praying and singing hymns to God, and the other prisoners were listening to them. Suddenly there was such a violent earthquake that the foundations of the prison were shaken. At once all the prison doors flew open, and everybody's chains came loose. The jailer woke up, and when he saw the prison doors open, he drew his sword and was about to kill himself because he thought the prisoners had escaped. But Paul shouted, "Don't harm yourself! We are all here!" The jailer called for lights, rushed in and fell trembling before Paul and Silas. He then brought them out and asked, "Sirs, what must I do to be saved?" They replied, "Believe in the Lord Jesus, and you will be saved—you and your household." Then they spoke the word of the Lord to him and to all the others in his house. At that hour of the night the jailer took them and washed their wounds; then immediately he and all his family were baptized. The jailer brought them into his house and set a meal before them; he was filled with joy because he had come to believe in God—he and his whole family. (Acts 16:25–34)

To Serve God in Serving Others

When it is difficult to serve; when the person we are to serve is difficult to please; or when we just don't feel like serving someone for any other reason, it is important to remember one simple truth:

When we serve others, we are actually serving God.

Every time we make an attempt to serve a demanding boss, an unappreciative patron, or an unlikable supervisor, the eventual success or failure of our efforts is not important. God is served when we serve those in our lives with authority over us. When, motivated by Jesus and His love, as we serve them and anyone else in our lives, we serve God.

Even the simplest act of sharpening a pencil or getting a cup of coffee becomes an act of devotion when we keep the perspective that our service for others is actually being done to glorify God.

React and Respond

1. Consider each of the following passages. Identify the characteristics of someone who serves God by serving others.

a. "Slaves, obey your earthly masters in everything; and do it, not only when their eye is on you and to win their favor, but with sincerity of heart and reverence for the Lord. Whatever you do, work at it with all your heart, as working for the Lord, not for men, since you know that you will receive an inheritance from the Lord as a reward. It is the Lord Christ you are serving" Colossians 3:22–24.

b. "Teach slaves to be subject to their masters in everything, to try to please them, not to talk back to them, and not to steal from them, but to show that they can be fully trusted, so that in every way they will make the teaching about God our Savior attractive" (Titus 2:9–10).

c. "Slaves, submit yourselves to your masters with all respect, not only to those who are good and considerate, but also to those who are harsh. For it is commendable if a man bears up under the pain of unjust suffering because he is conscious of God. But how is it to your credit if you receive a beating for doing wrong and endure it? But if you suffer for doing good and you endure it, this is commendable before God. To this you were called, because Christ suffered for you, leaving you an example, that you should follow in His steps. 'He committed no sin, and no deceit was found in His mouth' " (1 Peter 2:18–22).

2. What regard does God's Spirit bring to believers toward those in authority over them who are also believers?
All who are under the yoke of slavery should consider their masters worthy of full respect, so that God's name and our teaching may not be slandered. Those who have

believing masters are not to show less respect for them because they are brothers. Instead, they are to serve them even better, because those who benefit from their service are believers, and dear to them. These are the things you are to teach and urge on them, (1 Timothy 6:1–2).

3. Reflect on the message of each of the following for God's people who find themselves in positions of authority over others.

a. "Masters, provide your slaves with what is right and fair, because you know that you also have a Master in heaven" (Colossians 4:1).

b. "If I have denied justice to my menservants and maidservants when they had a grievance against me, what will I do when God confronts me? What will I answer when called to account? Did not He who made me in the womb make them? Did not the same One form us both within our mothers" (Job 31:13–15)?

c. "Do not take advantage of a hired man who is poor and needy, whether he is a brother Israelite or an alien living in one of your towns. Pay him his wages each day before sunset, because he is poor and is counting on it. Otherwise he may cry to the LORD against you, and you will be guilty of sin" (Deuteronomy 24:14–15).

d. If a ruler listens to lies, all his officials become wicked. (Proverbs 29:12)

I've Got You ... under My Skin

Whether we are bosses or employees, we all at times find ourselves in relationships that, for whatever reason, give us problems. Maybe it's a boss who can never be pleased. Or a co-worker who grates on our nerves, or speaks falsely about us behind our backs. Or an employee who doesn't do what he or she is told or is resentful of your authority. When we pray the Lord's Prayer, we ask our Father in heaven to enable us to forgive others as we have been forgiven and to forgive them from the heart.

React and Respond

1. What is the motivation for and result of a Christian's attitude of love and forgiveness?

> And He died for all, that those who live should no longer live for themselves but for Him who died for them and was raised again. (2 Corinthians 5:15)

2. In Matthew 18, Jesus provides us with a helpful procedure to follow if a fellow Christian has wronged us. This same procedure can also be applied in the workplace among believers and unbelievers alike. Explain the benefits of following this procedure for resolving conflicts at work.

> If your brother sins against you, go and show him his fault, just between the two of you. If he listens to you, you have won your brother over. But if he will not listen, take one or two others along, so that "every matter may be established by the testimony of two or three witnesses." If he refuses to listen to them, tell it to the church; and if he refuses to listen even to the church, treat him as you would a pagan or a tax collector. (Matthew 18:15–17)

To Bring Home the Bacon 5

God Provides

Grant loved his job. The people. The interesting and challenging work. The salary and benefits. For Grant the future looked bright and full of promise.

Until the one particularly cold, wintery day.

Grant was working in his office when Matt, another account executive, quietly and deliberately came in. Shutting the door behind him, Matt sat down in the chair next to Grant's desk.

"Listen, Grant. Are you aware of the rumors going around?"

Grant's thoughts raced back to a conversation he had had in the hallway with Sally just last week. Sally had told him management was looking to sell the firm. But a couple of days later, the president, himself, sat down with Grant and denied there was any truth to the rumors.

"Yes," Grant reluctantly answered Matt.

"Well, it's all true. Management's selling the firm ... and I'm here to tell you ... if Stevens hasn't contacted you ... you probably aren't going to make the cut."

Matt sank back in his chair a little, as if a great weight had been lifted off his chest. Brad Stevens was the owner of the other firm that was supposedly interested in acquiring Grant's company.

"But Bob denied this straight to my face. How could he do something like that?" Grant asked in disbelief.

"C'mon," Matt answered, "Bob would lie about anything if it meant more money in his pocket. You've worked with him before. You know what he's like."

"But, why would he lie to me?"

"Think about it. You do a lot around here. If you're gone, things would start breaking down. The company wouldn't be worth as much as when things were running on all cylinders.

Bob's a great manager, but even he can't keep this ship afloat if everyone's suddenly bailing on him. Face it, he used you. And now you've got to get out."

"How long, Matt?"

"I don't know … a couple of weeks, maybe. If you're lucky, maybe a month. Management's pretty greedy; I think they're holding out for as much as they can get. Let me know if I can do anything to help."

And then, as quickly as he had come in, Matt was gone.

Grant was left swimming in possibilities. Grant's pulse began to race as the gravity of the situation sank in. He and his wife had no real savings to speak of. If they were forced to do without income for any extended period of time, they would be in big trouble. His wife, Sally, was expecting their third child in July.

No sooner had thoughts of fear and unknown dread entered his mind, when a sudden rush of reassurance overtook him. Grant felt great relief. No matter what happened to him, he realized he can never be separated from the love of Christ. Grant was relatively new in his Christian faith and beliefs. The events at his work created an opportunity for him to test his faith. Grant remembered reading in Matthew, "So do not worry, saying, 'What shall we eat?' or 'What shall we drink?' or 'What shall we wear?' For the pagans run after all these things, and your heavenly Father knows that you need them. But seek first His kingdom and His righteousness, and all these things will be given to you as well" (Matthew 6:31–33).

Grant went back to this verse and reread it to himself. Reading on in chapter 7, Grant came across a special verse that really cheered him up: "Which of you, if his son asks for bread, will give him a stone? Or if he asks for a fish, will give him a snake? If you, then, though you are evil, know how to give good gifts to your children, how much more will your Father in heaven give good gifts to those who ask Him!" (Matthew 7:9–11).

Grant made a decision to take God at His Word. If God said it, it was good enough for him. He would not worry. He would do all that he could to look for another job. But he wholeheartedly believed that God knew what was best for him and would give him the right job at the right time.

The days that followed were long and hard. He sent out correspondences to as many people as he could, following up each letter and resume with a phone call. But today turned into tomorrow, days turned into weeks, and weeks became one month, then two.

He never knew how much time was left, but judging by Matt's earlier guesstimate, time was running out. One day Grant hit the wall. He felt spent, like he could go no further. He had done a great deal of work, but there were no fruits from his labor—his interview calendar for the coming week was empty. He fell to his knees in despair.

"Lord," he prayed, "please show me Your will. I know I can never be outside of it. I know You've promised to take care of me and my family. But I'm beginning to feel overwhelmed. Please help me. For the sake of Your Son, Jesus Christ."

His phone suddenly interrupted his prayer. It was someone wanting to set up an interview with him. No sooner had he hung up the phone when another call for another interview came in. Less than 15 minutes later, he noticed a message someone had written down with a vaguely familiar name on it. He slowly realized the person's name was the same one he'd written at the top of one the addresses of companies to whom he'd sent his resume. His heart leaped for joy when he called the number printed on the message and was met with a request for an interview.

Grant felt ecstatic with joy. Within 17 minutes of praying to God, Grant's interview calendar contained three appointments. More would follow. It was unmistakable. God had heard and answered Grant's prayers. Immediately. God was faithful. Indeed.

Three weeks went by. Grant had no solid job offers. He had been on six interviews in the last week. But nothing had happened. He was beginning to worry. He still didn't know how much time he had. So he prayed: Dear heavenly Father, I pray that something will happen soon. I don't have much time to go. I feel like a piece of cloth, dangling, twisting in the wind. But I trust in You. Like the man in the Bible who cries to Jesus, "Lord, I believe! Help me in my unbelief!" Grow my faith, Lord. Please take away my uncertainty. In Your Son's name I pray."

That very same week brought him three offers. And they were all excellent opportunities. God had saved him. He was faithful to His Word. Grant had a hard time narrowing it down to the best one. After he had accepted the top offer, he happily went to Bob to give him his official notice. His last day would be Wednesday.

Later, a couple of days before he started his new job, Grant was walking through the reception area when he heard a couple of his co-workers talking very dejectedly.

"Should we work half a day Wednesday and have a farewell party?" one asked.

Grant was puzzled; he got along well with these two colleagues, but not well enough for them to throw a farewell party in his honor.

Grant got the surprise of his life when he asked what was going on. Grant's co-workers were not talking about throwing a party in his honor. Wednesday, the same day that was scheduled to be Grant's last, was also to be the last day for the company. The sale had been finalized. The deal was done.

Grant rejoiced. The Lord had delivered him from unemployment. He felt that the angel of death had passed over his life. Grant felt a joy that must be related to what he expects to feel upon being raised from the dead by Jesus. And then he was overcome with thankfulness.

React and Respond

1. Do you agree or disagree with the following statement, "Most men find their identity in their work; while most women find their identity in their family and friends"? For whom or under what circumstances would loss of employment be especially difficult?

2. Not every Christian who faces the loss of his job and turns the situation over to God in prayer as Grant did, finds immediate employment with no loss of financial resources.

Many men of God struggle with extended periods of unemployment, income reduction, or financial ruin. But God invites us to turn our financial struggles and difficulties over to Him. He who went to the cross to pay the penalty our sins deserved has pledged always to remain with us to encourage and enable us with the promises of His Word.

Grant found Matthew 6:31–33 and Matthew 9:7–11 (printed earlier) especially meaningful during his time of frustration and disillusionment over his future. Would these verses have had the same significance for Grant had he faced a prolonged period of unemployment? Why or why not?

3. Old Testament king Jehoshaphat once faced a very stressful time in his career. Surrounded by a large invading force he prayed, "O our God, will You not judge them? For we have no power to face this vast army that is attacking us. We do not know what to do, but our eyes are upon You" (2 Chronicles 20:12).

a. What helpful insights does Jehoshaphat's prayer provide God's men of today as we face problems and difficulties in our lives?

b. God answered Jehoshaphat's prayer. He said: "Listen, King Jehoshaphat and all who live in Judah and Jerusalem! This is what the LORD says to you: 'Do not be afraid or discouraged because of this vast army. For the battle is not yours, but God's. Tomorrow march down against them. They will be climbing up by the Pass of Ziz, and you will find them at the end of the gorge in the Desert of Jeruel. You will not have to fight this battle. Take up your positions; stand firm and see the deliverance the LORD will give you, O Judah and Jerusalem. Do not be afraid; do not be discouraged. Go out to face them tomorrow, and the LORD will be with you'" (2 Chronicles 20:15–17).

Apply key phrases from God's words to Jehoshaphat to your life and the financial struggles and challenges you may face from time to time.

4. On a scale of 1–10 rate how close you feel to God during times of stress and extreme uncertainty. Is there a particular negative stressor in your life—job related or otherwise—that requires the strength God freely offers you? Why not talk to Him about it right now?

5. "At least we won't have to put up with work in heaven," quipped one man to the others assembled at a lunch-break Bible study. This comment set off a lengthy discussion about work and its place in God's plan for man.

"Well, Adam and Eve were given work to do in Eden before the fall into sin," someone responded.

"I'd rather look forward to heaven as a place of meaningful activity rather than as a place of rest. I hope there is work in heaven. I've found some of life's happiest and most fulfilling moments of my life at work when things are going well," added another.

Comment on this discussion. Do you think there will be work to do in heaven?

I Can Handle This

Self-sufficient, capable, strong. Throughout history, the human male has been idealized as the strong, silent provider; the breadwinner who can be counted on to venture out into the world to bring home the bacon at the end of the day. This stereotype has its roots in the most ancient of tribal societies.

Exposing themselves to unforeseen dangers, men would venture forth leaving the comforts of home to gather food for the entire tribe using the cunning, skill, and brut strength at their disposal. The women waiting for their return would honor their men as heroes.

But this image of masculinity becomes problematic when we start thanking our talents, abilities, and skills for our success in providing for ourselves and our families.

When we start looking at ourselves as the invincible breadwinner, we soon feel invincible. Stirrings of pride fill our hearts. When we have these types of feelings, we are in danger of losing proper perspective on things. Long ago Moses spoke to the people of Israel about the dangers of success. He said, "You may say to yourself, 'My power and the strength of my hands have produced this wealth for me.' But remember the LORD your God, for it is He who gives you the ability to produce wealth, and so confirms his covenant, which He swore to your forefathers, as it is today" (Deuteronomy 8:17–18).

When we are down and out with nowhere to turn, we may receive God's grace with great hunger and eagerness because by the power of the Holy Spirit we have been brought to recognize our great need and inadequacies. But then God's faithful times of fruitfulness and plenty hold a special risk.

When our bellies are full, when things are going well, when we have all that we need, we become most susceptible to a fall from grace. God Himself shares with Moses a simple, yet terrifying truth about mankind's true nature: "When I have brought them into the land flowing with milk and honey, the land I promised on oath to their forefathers, and when they eat their fill and thrive, they will turn to other gods and worship them, rejecting Me and breaking My covenant. And when many disasters and difficulties come upon them, this song will testify against them, because it will not be forgotten by their descendants. I know what they are disposed to do, even before I bring them into the land I promised them on oath" (Deuteronomy 31:20–21).

God knows what, when left on our own, we will do. Turn away from Him. He reaches out to us with a supreme love for us as individuals—even though He knows how hopelessly sinful we are. He knows every secret thing in your heart. And He knows everything about your faith in His Son. His is an unconditional love. We spend all of our new lives—lives His Spirit gives us through faith—trying to fathom that love.

When we turn our backs to God, we automatically turn to other gods (lower case "g")—Ourselves, Greed, Lust, Fear, Anger, Laziness, Jealousy, Relationships, Our Work, Sports, Hobbies—gods who preoccupy our minds and distract our focus on God. The sad thing is we are turning away from the one and only God who loves us more than we will ever know.

Though tempted to think otherwise, no man is ever really in charge of—or responsible for—anything. A man can get in trouble by thinking good fortune and career advancements and opportunities are self-made. Everything in life comes from a loving, righteous God. Everything: family, a job that pays for and economically sustains your family, abilities, and talents to perform your duties.

React and Respond

1. Apply Deuteronomy 31:20–21 to your life and times. What evidence of the gods that present a special temptation for those enjoying times of prosperity do you see in your life? in the world around you?

2. Have you seen the bumper sticker popular a few years ago that read: "The one with the most toys at the end of the game wins." Luke records a time when Jesus is teaching and one of two brothers in the crowd of listeners asks Jesus to tell his brother to share the inheritance. Jesus said, "Watch out! Be on your guard against all kinds of greed; a man's life does not consist of his possessions" (Luke 12:15). Jesus continues with a parable: "The ground of a certain rich man produced a good crop. He thought to himself, 'What shall I do? I have no place to store my crops.' Then he said, 'This is what I'll do. I will tear down my barns and build bigger ones, and there I will store all my grain and my goods. And I'll say to myself, "You have plenty of good things laid up in many years. Take life easy; eat, drink and be merry."' But God said to him, 'You fool! This very night your life will be demanded from you.

Then who will get what you have prepared for yourself?' This is how it will be with anyone who stores up things for himself but is not rich toward God" (Luke 12:16–21). What do you think it means to be rich toward God?

3. Read Proverbs 30:8–9. "Give me neither poverty nor riches, but give me only my daily bread. Otherwise, I may have too much and disown You and say, 'Who is the LORD?' Or I may become poor and steal, and so dishonor the name of my God."

Apply these verses to your life, contrasting your spiritual life during times of financial plenty with more lean times.

4. When the apostle Paul performs a miracle in Lystra, the surrounding crowd quickly call him and his partner Barnabas gods sent down from heaven. But Paul and Barnabas quickly identify themselves as mere men, humans like them. Then they made use of the opportunity to give credit to God—the source of all good things. "We are bringing you good news, telling you to turn from these worthless things to the living God, who made heaven and earth and sea and everything in them. In the past, He let all nations go their own way. Yet He has not left Himself without testimony: He has shown kindness by giving you rain from heaven and crops in their seasons; He provides you with plenty of food and fills your hearts with joy" (Acts 14:15–17).

What opportunities do the accomplishments in your life provide for you to talk about God and His good gifts to you through Christ Jesus?

5. In the Old Testament, God tells His people to rebuild the temple. As they were left to ponder this huge, seemingly insurmountable task, God tells them exactly where they were to draw their power and strength to accomplish this feat:

> So He said to me, "This is the word of the LORD to Zerubbabel: 'Not by might nor by power, but by My Spirit,' says the LORD Almighty." (Zechariah 4:6)

Apply these words to your life.

Under New Management

God has brought us to faith in Jesus. He has brought us to the realization that in Jesus our sins of financial obsession and all others are gone—removed when Jesus died for them some 2000 years ago, suspended on a cruel wooden cross on a Palestinian hillside. He has made us new. As His new men, we have received through His Holy Spirit a new life complete with a new identity and a new sense of direction. We are the men of God; we have a higher, more worthy, and certainly more exciting set of goals in life than the accumulation of toys. God has brought us under new management—His. When God comes into a man's heart, things change. As His Spirit comes to us through God's Word, we desire to serve God through cheerful, selfless, and generous sharing of the blessings He has given to us. We learn how to do this from God Himself.

As our relation with God grows through faith in Jesus we desire to become more like Him. God loves a cheerful giver because He is the most cheerful and most generous of all givers—He gives us everything we have, everything we need—including and most important, faith and a new life through His Son, Jesus Christ.

In His Word God provides us with helpful insights about the blessings of generous, cheerful, and selfless giving.

64

React and Respond

1. God's Word encourages us with the fact that we don't have to be rich in order to give generously. Mark 12:41–44 records, "Jesus sat down opposite the place where the offerings were put and watched the crowd putting their money into the temple treasury. Many rich people threw in large amounts. But a poor widow came and put in two very small copper coins, worth only a fraction of a penny. Calling His disciples to Him, Jesus said, 'I tell you the truth, this poor widow has put more into the treasury than all the others. They gave out of their wealth; but she, out of her poverty, put in everything—all she had to live on.'"

a. God gives generosity to us. How is His generosity to the widow reflected in her gift to Him?

b. As the Holy Spirit works in the hearts and lives of God's men, how can great wealth be a great resource?

2. Oh, what a joy to be loved by the God who created heaven and earth and yet loved us enough to give us an indescribable gift—His only Son to be our Savior and Friend and Lord. 2 Corinthians 9:6–15 speaks to us about the joy of giving. "Remember this: Whoever sows sparingly will also reap sparingly, and whoever sows generously will also reap generously. Each man should give what he has decided in his heart to give, not reluctantly or under compulsion, for God loves a cheerful giver. And God is able to make all grace abound to you, so that in all things at all times, having all that you need, you will abound in every good work. As it is written: 'He has scattered abroad His gifts to the poor; His righteousness endures forever.' Now He who supplies seed to the sower and bread for food will also supply and increase your store of seed and will enlarge the harvest of your righteousness. You will

be made rich in every way so that you can be generous on every occasion, and through us your generosity will result in thanksgiving to God. This service that you perform is not only supplying the needs of God's people but is also overflowing in many expressions of thanks to God. Because of the service by which you have proved yourselves, men will praise God for the obedience that accompanies your confession of the gospel of Christ, and for your generosity in sharing with them and with everyone else. And in their prayers for you their hearts will go out to you, because of the surpassing grace God has given you. Thanks be to God for His indescribable gift!"

a. The joy of giving is a mysterious joy that God's Spirit brings. What reasons for joy do you find in these verses?

b. Relate the last sentence in the above selection from 2 Corinthians 9 to those preceding it.

Opportunities and Adventures

God has planned amazing things for each person who belongs to Him. Into these lives He brings countless opportunities to share the Good News of Jesus and other blessings with others. At times, though, our lives are like a puzzle. We can't understand why God sends or permits to be sent the adventures that come our way. We may question why we have relatively few financial resources and limited career opportunities while the ungodly seem to have abundant money, connections, potentialities.

No matter what challenges we may face in our lives—financial, career-related, or other, we know that God has our best interests at heart. He has promised to continue to give us responsibilities and resources to use for Him. Plus He invites us to continue coming to Him in prayer asking for His continued blessings according to His will. James reminds us "You do not have, because you do not ask God" (James 4:2).

God desires to bless His people so that they in return may be a blessing to others. Martin Luther's wife, Katie, once gently chided him for his generosity toward others. Luther's answer reminds us of who God is and how He loves and cares for His people. "God is rich," Luther said, "He will give us more!"

REACT AND RESPOND

1. Jesus once said, "No one can serve two masters. Either he will hate the one and love the other, or he will be devoted to the one and despise the other. You cannot serve both God and Money" (Matthew 6:24). Give examples of how men of God show their regard for God over and above their love of money.

2. Paul writes to believers at Philippi, "I know what it is to be in need, and I know what it is to have plenty. I have learned the secret of being content in any and every situation, whether well fed or hungry, whether living in plenty or in want. I can do everything through Him who gives me strength" (Philippians 4:12–13). What exactly was Paul's source of contentment?

Apply Paul's words to your life and ambitions.

6 CAN YOU SPARE SOME CHANGE?

LETTERS TO MOM

27 September 1972

Dear Mom:

"Mine eyes have seen the glory!"

Mom, I wish you could have been here for the miracle of Timmy's birth. It was incredible. Laura, as you might expect, took it lying down (ha-ha), but was a real trooper. I am very proud of her and amazed at this wonderful gift of new life. Now I know what you must have felt like when Jack and I were born.

He's just perfect, Mom! 8 lbs., 6 oz. and 22 inches of roly-poly joy. He's got dark black hair like Dad and the strongest little grip.

Laura's water broke on Sunday night. She was in labor all day Monday. We waited and waited, but Laura didn't dilate more than four centimeters—not even half enough for the delivery. The doctor (Dr. Richard Kramer—a very nice man) was more patient in waiting for this baby than I was.

Finally, Dr. Kramer had had enough, and late Monday (5:15 P.M. to be exact) he decided to take little Timmy C-section. They made me wait outside the whole time. I must've paced a four-foot ditch in that waiting room. I was nearly sick to my stomach, worrying for Laura and the baby, that something might go wrong. I was praying harder than I think I've ever prayed before (I know it's important to you). And God certainly answered all of my prayers ... and then some.

He's so cute! What a blessing this little baby is to all of us! Now I now what it feels like to have "my cup running over!" God is good, Mother, just like you've always said.

Work's going great! I was promoted to regional sales director for the entire Midwest region (our biggest producing region!). I have some great ideas on how to make the company run smoother and more efficiently. We need great ideas too because if we don't make some changes soon, our competitors will eat us alive. Sometimes I wonder what management is thinking. I just wish I were calling the shots.

So when are you and Dad going to come visit and meet this new grandson of yours? Laura and I would love to see the two of you if Dad can ever pull himself away from his work. It would be perfect if you could make it this Thanksgiving! Hope to hear from you soon.

I love you.

Your son, Charles

React and Respond

1. Can you identify with Charles at his stage of life? What kinds of things are important to him? What are his hopes? goals? dreams?

2. Apply Psalm 127, printed as follows, to Charles and all young men as they think about and plan their future.

> Unless the LORD builds the house, its builders labor in vain. Unless the LORD watches over the city, the watchmen stand guard in vain. In vain you rise early and stay up late, toiling for food to eat—for He grants sleep to those He loves. Sons are a heritage from the LORD, children a reward from Him. Like arrows in the hands of a warrior are sons born in one's youth. Blessed is the man whose quiver is full of them. They will not be put to shame when they contend with their enemies in the gate.

3. Leaders in evangelism recognize life events, such as marriage or the birth of children, as ideal times for talking with people about their spiritual life. Why do you suppose this is so?

12 February 1992

Dear Mom:

Sorry I haven't written to you sooner, but I've been real busy. It's not easy being this city's Entrepreneur of the Year and owner of the hottest new company in the United States! I hope you're proud of me, Mom. Things are going really well.

Starting my own company was the smartest thing I've ever done. I'm doing everything I wanted to do at my old job, and I'm getting paid to be the boss. Can you believe it, Mom? I'm the boss.

The orders just keep coming in. In fact, we're having problems keeping up with all of them. We just landed the Martin-Helix account, which we've been pursuing for a long time now. Adding that business just quadrupled the size of my company. Could it get any better than this? I'm thankful for all the smarts and abilities I inherited (and the good looks you and Dad gave me too)!

Little Timmy's doing well—only he's not so little anymore. I've got him working in the new business (Wasn't it just yesterday he took his first steps?). You'd be proud of him. I know I am. It's my hope that Timmy can take over all of this someday. He'll do a great job.

It's such a great feeling knowing I'm building something significant with my own two hands. Something that provides food, clothing, shelter, and much, much more for my family. It warms my heart knowing I'm building a legacy for Timmy to continue when I retire. I know you said I should be thankful to God for all that's happened to me, and I do thank Him. Still I couldn't be a success without hours and hours of hard work. I like the saying, pray with one hand and put cash in the other and see which one you fill up first.

I'm been having a difficult time with Laura lately. I can't quite figure her out. I give her everything she wants, and still she says she's not happy. Dozens of women would kill to be my wife; I think she takes me for granted. It seems like she doesn't know what she wants. Maybe after all these years, you were right about her, Mom, but I hope not. How about calling her and giving her one of your famous "pep talks"? I know if anyone can bring her out of this, it's you, Mom. Please see what you can do.

I'll be in your neck of the woods next month. How about if

I stop in there and visit you and Dad? How's his health? Has he gotten rid of that cough? Anyway, maybe you could treat me to a famous batch of your chicken and dumplings. I'll call you in a couple of days to fill you in on the details.

I love you.

Your son, Charles

REACT AND RESPOND

4. Evaluate Charles in each of the following roles:

a. child of God

b. husband

c. father

d. worker

e. son

5. What danger exists when we experience success? Consider the following:

> Be careful that you do not forget the LORD your God, failing to observe His commands, His laws and His decrees .... Otherwise, when you eat and are satisfied, when you build fine houses and settle down, and when your herds and flocks grow large and your silver and gold increase and all you have is multiplied, then your heart will become proud and you will forget the LORD your God, who brought you out of Egypt, out of the land of slavery. ... You may say to yourself, "My power and the strength of my hands have produced this wealth for me." But remember the LORD your God, for it is He who gives you the ability to produce wealth, and so confirms His covenant, which He swore to your forefathers, as it is today. If you ever forget the LORD your God and follow other gods and worship and bow down to them, ... you will surely be destroyed." (Deuteronomy 8:11–19)

6. What direction does God provide us in His Word for those times when we feel the burden of the sins of self-reliance and disregard for God?

> The blood of Jesus, His Son, purifies us from all sin. If we claim to be without sin, we deceive ourselves and the truth is not in us. If we confess our sins, He is faithful and just and will forgive us our sins and purify us from all unrighteousness. (1 John 1:7–9)

18 October 1996
Dear Mom:
I swear, I didn't see it coming.

The Martin-Helix account was growing with us so much that suddenly they were 70% of our business. How stupid can I get? In the back of my mind, I knew I had to get some stuff cooking on new business, but Martin-Helix was eating up all of my time—it was eating up the time of most of my employees.

The beginning of the end was when they hired that snot-nosed Harvard Wudkind—the marketing genius who was going to bring Martin-Helix back to its glory days—Man, I've got ties older than this guy. We spent four good years servicing that account and what did it get us? That punk even had the gall to send us a letter terminating our relationship. Not even a phone call, Mom. You'd think four years of working together would merit a face-to-face explanation. I guess in his mind, it didn't.

The end of all I've worked so hard for is near. I'm keeping this place running with smoke and mirrors. When I go home at night, I can't ever get to sleep. I toss and turn all night. I'm haunted by dreams about my real-life nightmare. As if going through this mess isn't bad enough, I have to dream about it too. Why is God putting me through this? I can barely drag myself out of bed to go in in the morning. I'm losing all my best employees; they're not stupid, they can see the writing on the wall. We're dying. It's only a matter of time.

Timmy left last month. That was the hardest thing I've ever been through. I know it wasn't easy for him. He felt like a rat deserting a sinking ship, like he was giving up on his old man. But I can't blame him. There's no future for him here. No legacy. No hope. Besides the offer he got was a great one. I would've taken it myself if it had been offered to me.

Laura's been a great comfort to me in this time of trial. But even her reassurances can't stop me from feeling like an idiot. I'm a complete, total failure. I walk into my office and I feel like all eyes are on me. My ears burn when they whisper about my shortsightedness and inability to turn my company out of its dive.

Mom, please say a prayer to God for me. Ask Him why He's putting me through this misery, this living hell on earth. I need all the help I can get.

I'll call you soon. I've got to go. I love you.

Your son, Charles

React and Respond

7. How would you describe Charles' attitude toward God reflected in this letter to his mother?

8. God works in hearts of those who are ready to receive Him, who acknowledge their need for His help and recognize their inability to handle things on their own. Do you think Charles has reached this point in his life?

9. What does Jesus desire to bring to Charles and all others like Him? [Jesus said] "Come to Me, all you who are weary and burdened, and I will give you rest. Take My yoke upon you and learn from Me, for I am gentle and humble in heart, and you will find rest for your souls" (Matthew 11:28–29).

12 December 1996
Dear Mom:
I didn't think my life could get any worse. But it did.

I don't know how to tell you this, so I'm just going to say it: Laura's left me. She said she couldn't stand being married to me anymore. She said she felt like she was suffocating. She kicked me while I was down, Mom. I will never forgive her for what she's done to me.

I'm all alone now. I don't see how I'll ever crawl out from the debt incurred in my business failings. I've had to change my personal phone number three times because people keep calling when they get my number trying to get their money out of me—as if I've got any to give them. And now this.

I thought I was doing a good job with Laura. I wanted everything to work out. Sure, we had our shaky moments, but don't all marriages? You and Dad, I know, had your share of arguments. But through it all, I wanted it to work like your marriage did. We even saw a counselor. I found out later that the counselor was talking to Laura behind my back, telling her that the relationship was already over and instructing her on the "50 Ways to Leave Your Lover."

I know you feel strongly about God and stuff, but if there is a God, why is He putting me through all this garbage? Doesn't He know how much I've already suffered? Aren't good things supposed to happen to good people? I'm a good person; you know that, Mom. I never cheated on Laura, never even really had time to. I never stole or killed anybody. So why is God out to get me? Was it something I did? Was it something I didn't do?

I don't know how much longer I can go on. Most days I don't leave the house. Some days I don't even leave my bed. I need to hear from you, Mom. I need you to tell me everything's going to be okay. Please call me as soon as you can.

With love, Charles

React and Respond

10. What two possible outcomes could result as Charles struggles with his unhappiness and disappointments?

"Godly sorrow brings repentance that leads to salvation and leaves no regret, but worldly sorrow brings death" (2 Corinthians 7:10).

11. What does God give to all who by the power of the Holy Spirit repent, trusting in Jesus and the payment for sin

and new beginning He earned for us in His life, death, and resurrection?

"Repent, then, and turn to God, so that your sins may be wiped out, that times of refreshing may come from the Lord" (Acts 3:19).

12. All who come to Jesus for a new beginning receive far more than they could ever expect. Use the following words of Paul to describe the new life God offers to those who enter His family through faith in Christ Jesus.

a. "What, then, shall we say in response to this? If God is for us, who can be against us? He who did not spare His own Son, but gave Him up for us all—how will He not also, along with Him, graciously give us all things" (Romans 8:31–32)?

b. "I know what it is to be in need, and I know what it is to have plenty. I have learned the secret of being content in any and every situation, whether well fed or hungry, whether living in plenty or in want. I can do everything through Him who gives me strength" (Philippians 4:12–13).

c. "Godliness with contentment is great gain" (1 Timothy 6:6).

New Beginnings

Our God is a God of new beginnings. When He leads us to a realization of our sinfulness and brings us to a saving faith in Jesus our Savior, He frees us allowing us to leave the sinfulness of our past behind us and to accept and grow in the freedom of new choices and opportunities He so generously provides.

Long ago God gave the same freedom to His chosen people who had been in bondage for 430 years in Egypt. Under the leadership of Moses God promised deliverance to His people. He said, "I am the LORD, and I will bring you out from under the yoke of the Egyptians. I will free you from being slaves to them, and I will redeem you with an outstretched arm and with mighty acts of judgment, I will take you as My own people, and I will be your God" (Exodus 6:6–7a).

Later, after God freed Israel from their oppressors, God's people found themselves longing for the safety and security of their former life. Like animals sitting contently in open cages, the people of Israel shied away from the new freedom God had already given them. To Moses they complained, "Was it because there were no graves in Egypt that you brought us to the desert to die? What have you done to us by bringing us out of Egypt? Didn't we say to you in Egypt, 'Leave us alone; let us serve the Egyptians'? It would have been better for us to serve the Egyptians than to die in the desert!" (Exodus 14:11–12).

React and Respond

1. When we became Christians, we underwent a dramatic change. Like the apostle Paul whose meeting with Jesus left His life forever changed, when we came to faith, the Spirit of God transformed us from enemies of God to God's children through Christ Jesus. When do you find yourself longing for the comfort of the old, natural life which was yours before you came to faith?

2. The devil, the world, and natural sinful human desires remain at work in the life of every person who has become a child of God, trying to convince us that the new life in Christ isn't worth the sacrifice or that it simply doesn't exist. What help do we have in living the new life?

> Praise be to the God and Father of our Lord Jesus Christ! In His great mercy He has given us new birth into a living hope through the resurrection of Jesus Christ from the dead, and into an inheritance that can never perish, spoil or fade—kept in heaven for you, who through faith are shielded by God's power until the coming of the salvation that is ready to be revealed in the last time. (1 Peter 1:3–5)

3. As God's power displays itself in our lives by the working of the Holy Spirit through the Word of God
   a. how will we as men of God relate to the world around us?

> Dear friends, I urge you, as aliens and strangers in the world, to abstain from sinful desires, which war against your soul. Live such good lives among the pagans that, though they accuse you of doing wrong, they may see your good deeds and glorify God on the day He visits us." (1 Peter 2:11–12)

   b. how can we combat the forces that urge us to return to our former way of life?

> You, dear children, are from God and have overcome them, because the One who is in you is greater than the one who is in the world. (1 John 4:4)

Facing Change

No matter how different we may be from one another, one common force affects us all: change. Things change. People change. Lives change. Sometimes we long for change, hoping for better things. At other times we resist change especially when it carries with it a note of uncertainty or appears on the surface to be unpleasant. But men of God have nothing to fear. God promises to go with us through each new challenge of each new day. And we can depend on Him and on His promises because He never changes.

We can trust in Jesus' desire to remain with us to help and encourage us along life's way because He paid the ultimate price for us though it cost Him His very life. He has promised to ride the storms of life with us reminding us of His presence and power just as He did for His disciples one day long ago when they rode together on the rough waters of the Galilean Sea.

Without warning, a furious storm came up on the lake, so that the waves swept over the boat. But Jesus was sleeping. The disciples went and woke Him, saying, "Lord, save us! We're going to drown!"

He replied, "You of little faith, why are you so afraid?" Then He got up and rebuked the winds and the waves, and it was completely calm. (Matthew 8:24–26)

As we face life's changes, both positive and negative, we may at times become overcome with fear. But again God assures us of His desire to influence the daily exercise of the new lives we live for Him. The apostle John writes, "God is love. Whoever lives in love lives in God, and God in him. In this way, love is made complete among us so that we will have confidence on the day of judgment, because in this world we are like Him. There is no fear in love. But perfect love drives out fear" (1 John 4:16b–18a).

The perfect love of God can help overcome our fear of anything, including life without a loved one, uncertainty, failure, other people, even death.

REACT AND RESPOND

1. How do you feel about the change? Has change been a friend or foe in your life? Explain.

2. Name some change in your life that you have recently gone through. It may be big or it may be small. If it was important to you, that's all that counts. Did you feel this change was forced upon you or was it something you had a choice about? How did you perceive it before it happened? while you were going through it? How do you perceive it now as you reflect back on it?

3. Why do you think God allows us to go through situations that cause stress in our lives? Why do you think He allows us to experience the anxiety of uncertainty? Consider the following.

78

In this you greatly rejoice, though now for a little while you may have had to suffer grief in all kinds of trials. These have come so that your faith—of greater worth than gold, which perishes even though refined by fire—may be proved genuine and may result in praise, glory and honor when Jesus Christ is revealed. (1 Peter 1:6–7)

God at Work

The life of every follower of Jesus has God at work in it. As we read and study His Word and as we receive it together with our brothers and sisters in Christ assembled with us around our Lord's Table, God strengthens us for a new life lived for Him. As Jesus strengthens and encourages us in our new life of beginnings and changes, we can approach new experiences and relationship in both our personal and professional lives confident of our ultimate success as sons of God.

"We don't know what the future holds," someone once quipped. "But we know who holds the future." And for those who belong to Jesus the future holds events and experiences so great and wonderful we can't even imagine them. God's Word declares, "No eye has seen, no ear has heard, no mind has conceived what God has prepared for those who love Him" (1 Corinthians 2:9).

For centuries men of God have found strength and comfort in Psalm 23. Read this psalm now as you think about the changes facing you at work, at home, or in the lives of those around you.

The LORD is my shepherd, I shall not be in want. He makes me lie down in green pastures, He leads me beside quiet waters, He restores my soul. He guides me in paths of righteousness for His name's sake. Even though I walk through the valley of the shadow of death, I will fear no evil, for You are with me; Your rod and Your staff, they comfort me. You prepare a table before me in the presence of my enemies. You anoint my head with oil; my cup overflows. Surely goodness and love will follow me all the days of my life, and I will dwell in the house of the LORD forever.

React and Respond

1. What do the words, "I shall not be in want" mean to you in your life and situation?

2. In what ways does Jesus make you lie down in green pastures, lead you beside quiet waters, and restore your soul?

3. What are the paths of righteousness? What stake does God have in our walking "in paths of righteousness"?

4. When God's power comes into the lives of men of God, amazing things happen. On the basis of the following verses, suggest an appropriate philosophy of life to carry with you into the future. "Therefore, since we are surrounded by such a great cloud of witnesses, let us throw off everything that hinders and the sin that so easily entangles, and let us run with perseverance the race marked out for us. Let us fix our eyes on Jesus, the author and perfecter of our faith, who for the joy set before Him endured the cross, scorning its shame, and sat down at the right hand of the throne of God" (Hebrews 12:1–2).

5. As you think about facing the changes certain to confront you at work and in every other aspect of your life, tell what the following words of Paul mean to you, "Now to Him who is able to do immeasurably more than all we ask or imagine, according to His power that is at work within us, to Him be glory in the church and in Christ Jesus throughout all generations, for ever and ever! Amen" (Ephesians 3:20–21).

Answers and Comments

Finding Meaning and Purpose

One Man's Tragedy

React and Respond

1. Answers will vary. Generally, most of us hope our positive perceptions of ourselves are shared by those around us and that our "darker side" is able to be contained so that others—including those closest to us—do not come to regard us in a mostly negative light. Only God truly knows us; He knows us even better than we know ourselves. And He loves us anyway.

2a. Stories of desperation and disillusionment abound. God has a better plan for us. His desire for us extends beyond our freedom from sin, death, and the devil. He came so that we may have life and "have it to the full" (John 10:10).

b. Without Christ all of us are in the most hopeless and desperate of straits. Each of us has the potential for rejecting God and His saving grace. Affirm the power and strength God provides to us and all people as His Holy Spirit works faith in us through the Word of God.

c. Invite responses but do not force anyone to share.

3. *Man's failure is God's opportunity*—Only when we recognize the hopelessness of our lives without God are we ready to receive the Good News of the salvation Jesus has already won for us.

He does not remember sweet things who has not tasted bitter things—Like clouds before sunshine, the grace of God shines brightly in lives newly won from the clutches of darkness, as the zeal and enthusiasm of recent converts bears witness.

Wash me, and I will be whiter than snow (Psalm 51:7b)—Jesus has completely removed the penalty of our sins through the ultimate price He paid for us on Calvary's cruel, wooden cross.

4–5. When we or those we know feel overwhelmed under the burden of sin and its consequences, we can be reminded of God's love and promises. Jesus went to the cross to pay the

81

penalty our sins deserved. He will strengthen us with His power and "restore [us in] the joy of [His] salvation" (Psalm 51:12). We need not remain in our despair; Jesus rebuilds broken lives. (See Matthew 11:28–29.)

True Value

React and Respond

1. Share thoughts about how you feel when someone asked you what you do for a living. Many men who are going through a period of unemployment, especially dread being asked questions about work. Some will even try to keep unemployment a secret. Explore other ways we tend to associate ourselves and our worth with our occupation. Experts say that traditionally men are likely to discuss work with new acquaintances, whereas woman are more inclined to talk with those they have recently met about relationships and family issues.

2. As God in Christ has made people new, He takes our brokenness and builds a new man, someone who belongs to Him possessing a new sense of purpose, priorities, and goals. As His Holy Spirit works in our hearts through the power of God's Word, we look upon others, not according to how they look or who they are, but as fellow sinners for whom Christ died and rose again.

3. Share examples of how God works in natural forces and in the events and occurrences of daily life to remind us that He is in control. See also James 4:13–15. In addition to getting our attention, God also provides us with opportunities to share the Good News of Jesus with others through the course of our professional and private lives.

A View of Vocations

React and Respond

1. Possibilities are not limited to but may include social aspects, monetary rewards, personal fulfillment, opportunity to make a significant contribution.

2. In our world we benefit from the degree of specialization that God has allowed to occur to coincide with our high standard of living. As each member of society contributes a beneficial product or service, the whole of society improves, just as, using the analogy of the body, God's people benefit from encouraging and supporting one another in the diversity of gifts God has provided.

Our Work, His Perspective

React and Respond

1. Every day we are blessed by efforts and resources contributed by those who do not yet believe in Jesus as their Savior. A biblical comparison would be the people of Egypt before the Exodus who presented the people of Israel with their wealth just before they left Egypt to journey to the Promised Land.

2. By the power and motivation the Holy Spirit works in us, we can serve God by giving our best effort to our work as a service to God and as a witness to those around us of the hope we have in Christ Jesus our Lord.

In Search of a True Definition

React and Respond

1. God desires those who belong to Him to work. He provides us with the raw materials and resources necessary to find fulfillment and meaning in our life's work.

2. Through God's Word the Holy Spirit motivates and empowers. Share and listen as others share examples of God's watchful hand upon both the professional and private lives of His people.

Finding Time

Slip Sliding Away

React and Respond

1. Answers will vary. God invites us to bring these and all other concerns to Him in prayer. By the Spirit's power we will find as Paul did, "I can do everything through Him who gives me strength" (Philippians 4:13). We can also share our frustrations with trusted Christian friends who will help us to keep our problems in perspective. Life's worries, riches, and pleasures do indeed choke the life out of our relationship with Jesus Christ. By looking at the things that create impasses in our spiritual walk, we can take steps to remove the obstacles to our faith. Through the day-to-day choices we make, we determine what is important in our lives. Sometimes, two or more "important areas" of our lives will be in conflict. It's

important to do the best we can and let God take care of the rest. The thing to remember is that we don't have to be Supermen and accomplish everything. The important battle has already been won for us by Christ's death and resurrection.

2. God always hears our prayers and cries for mercy. In times of struggle or frustration, it's sometimes helpful to remember the times when God demonstrated His faithfulness to us in especially powerful ways just as He did before David went into battle with Goliath. There are a number of reasons someone might keep a problem from God. One of them is that we feel in the grand scheme of things, the problem is not very important. But the wonderful truth of the matter is that if something's important to us, it's important to God. Our concerns are His concerns. He promises always to listen to our prayers.

3. Invite participants to share comments and reflections, but do not force anyone to share.

It's about Time

React and Respond

1. Invite comments from the group. Affirm the concept that God is more than capable of handling any problem or concern that troubles or burdens us.

2. We all, at one time or another, have put the love of riches and worldly comforts before God. Allow time for participants to write three items and reflect on the strain they present to their relationship with God.

3a. Accept responses.

b. The comfort in 1 John 5:3–5 lies in the fact that no matter what we do or don't do, no matter what we accomplish or fail at, Christ has already overcome the world and its challenges and troubles for us. The struggles we go through as we attempt to live the Christian life are put into perspective when we consider Christ's work for us on the cross.

c. Our Savior and Lord enables us to use all the things He has given us to His glory and for the expansion of His kingdom. Invite participants to share specific examples from their lives.

God's Time, Not Ours

React and Respond

1a. The important things, the things of lasting significance, are related to God and His work, not our own work. We can take comfort in the fact that our relationship with God cannot be taken away from us by anyone or anything. Even though there is nothing that can take away our faith, we sometimes let it slip out of our hands. Ask the men in your group to remember a time when they fell away from the faith for a period of time. What made them fall away? Your answers will vary. It most likely will be because of a time when things were going good rather than a difficult time. Other answers may include various distractions or modern-day diversions.

b. We can be rich toward God by the power of the Holy Spirit working within us as we read, study, and meditate upon God's Word and partake of the Sacrament. His power will enable us to serve Him in keeping with His will for our lives.

2. When Jesus supported His disciples' action of picking and eating grain on the Sabbath, He affirmed that we also honor God by tending to the needs of our bodies.

3. When we receive God's Word, by the Spirit's power it begins to work its life-changing effect in us.

The Inevitable Fruit

React and Respond

1. The grace of God has appeared to all men as the Good News of Jesus is shared with all people everywhere.

2. When God's power enables us to break the cycle of sin in our lives, the devil's work is destroyed and God is glorified. What cycle of sin in your life could you concentrate on and make a priority of breaking? How would this glorify God?

3. Invite participants to share specific examples.

Guiding Principles

React and Respond

1. What we do as a response to all that God in Christ has done for us is of eternal value. Christ will comment on these evidences of our faith when He welcomes us into heaven with the words, "Well done, good and faithful servant! (Matthew 25:21) ... Whatever you did for one of the least of these brothers of Mine, you did for Me" (Matthew 25:40).

2. We honor God by living a balanced life in which He is the Lord. By being balanced we are able to divide ourselves between God, family, work, and other responsibilities and obligations and still be available for the unique opportunities to be God's servant which He will provide for us.

How Well Do You Do Your Living?

A Matter of Integrity

React and Respond

1. Encourage others to share. If necessary, prime the pump with your willingness to share your experience relating it to each of the following passages.

a. Sinfulness is innate in each of us as David describes (Psalm 51:5).

b. Recognition of our sinfulness can prepare our hearts for God's presence as the Holy Spirit shows us our need for Jesus, the Savior (2 Corinthians 7:10).

c. Jesus took our sins upon Himself. In taking our sins upon Himself, He gave us His righteousness in the trade (2 Corinthians 5:21).

2a. We know that being honest is the right and proper way to live because God has written His Law on each human heart (Romans 2:13–15).

b. God would have His people deal honestly with all others. He forbids any process, creative or otherwise, in which others are cheated (Deuteronomy 25:13–16).

c. "Honest scales and balances are from the LORD" (Proverbs 16:11). Perfect justice is an attribute of God. Our sense of it comes from Him. Dealing honestly with others is one way to show the presence of God in our lives.

3a. Out of a desire to show the difference Jesus' presence was making in his life, Zacchaeus (Luke 19:8) pledged a generous donation to the disadvantaged together with a promise to restore four times any amount he had cheated anyone. Zacchaeus wanted people to see God's power and love evidenced mightily in his life.

b. Answers will vary. Encourage sharing of examples of Zacchaeus-style, Spirit-driven actions of Christian witness.

Jungle Warfare

React and Respond

1a. Encourage participants to share examples of the prowling of the devil (lion) in their lives.

b. We can help our brothers "throughout the world who are undergoing the same kind of sufferings" by supporting and encouraging them in the Gospel through our words, actions, and prayers on their behalf. See also Hebrews 10:19–25.

2. Encourage participants with the assurance that God is the only true source of strength and encouragement in the daily spiritual battles that assail us.

a. God promises to protect us with the assurance of our salvation and to strengthen us with the Word of God (Ephesians 6:11, 17).

b. Jesus understands the fearsome pull of temptations in a man's life; He endured them Himself, yet without giving in (Hebrews 4:14–16). Jesus our Savior invites us to give our problems and temptations over to Him. He will help us carry our burdens and will give us peace in our struggles (Matthew 11:28–29).

c. Many of us have belonged to God by faith in Christ Jesus for many years. God promises to continue His life-renewing work in us, strengthening our faith as His Spirit works in our lives through the Word of God (Philippians 1:6).

d. We can find joy in our struggles knowing that God is at work in our lives, nurturing our relationship with Him (James 1:2–3).

An Example of Integrity

React and Respond

1. When we work to be effective in our chosen profession as a way of bringing honor and glory to God, whether or not anyone notices is of little importance. Nothing passes the watchful eye of our loving God.

2. God promises not to allow us to be tempted beyond what we can bear. He will remain by our side at all times including times of temptation (1 Corinthians 10:13).

3. Answers will vary.

a. Setbacks remind us of our need for God. We can praise and thank Him for His continual presence and care in our lives.

b. We praise God when at the height of our glory we channel praise for our accomplishments and achievements toward God. After all, our talents, time, and circumstances are all graciously given to us by Him.

c. We can share our feelings with God and trust in His

ability to give us peace during those times when we feel (perhaps as Joseph did) that we are not treated fairly at the hands of others.

Forward into Battle

React and Respond

1. Answers will vary. Encourage participants to share.

2. Most likely, Mark realized that where his words and actions toward his co-workers were concerned, he was not showing others the presence of Jesus in His life. Mark's spiritual struggle involves relying on the power of the Holy Spirit to change His way of relating with those with whom he works. Comment that a dynamic change in Mark's life is likely to be noticed by others. Their curiosity about the change in Mark may provide him with the opportunity to witness. St. Peter encourages us, "But in your hearts set apart Christ as Lord. Always be prepared to give an answer to everyone who asks you to give the reason for the hope that you have. But do this with gentleness and respect" (1 Peter 3:15).

3. Accept participants' answers. Pray for the life-changing power in your life and in the lives of other men in your group.

A Good and Faithful Worker

A Struggle with Obedience

React and Respond

1. Especially in times of war, obedience to a superior officer is vitally important. God's forgiveness covers all wrong choices, including those involving the loss of human lives.

2. Again accept responses. Sometimes a difficult choice must be made between submitting to the authority of those placed over us and expending energy to keep ourselves and others from doing things we know to be wrong and carrying serious consequences.

3. Peter and John maintain the perspective that Christians must answer to God before we answer to other authori-

ties. Like other heroes of faith throughout the history of Christendom, they were unwilling to compromise in order that the Good News of Jesus might be proclaimed unhindered and unrestrained.

4a. Our primary Christian mission as we await our Savior's return to is bring the Gospel to all who do not yet believe, including persons in our families, in our neighborhoods, and throughout the world. Focusing on this objective helps the people of God keep things in perspective when decisions need to be made.

b. All people witness to their belief system, whether they are conscious of it or not. Therefore, every issue to which we respond affects our Christian witness. At times taking an unpopular stand for the sake of the Gospel of Jesus will better help others to know and understand us and the Lord we serve. At other times, faithful service to an unappreciative and even unkind person offers on opportunity to glorify God.

SERVICE

React and Respond

1. Answers will vary. Examples of company professional loyalty still exist. However, many in today's workforce move frequently from job to job, or company to company, sometimes even changing careers.

2a. God has established the authorities in our world to preserve order and provide protection and security for His people.

b. Those to whom we report have a vital role in helping us secure the resources we need to provide for ourselves and our families. They enable us to do our tasks well to the glory of God and for the welfare of others. Good supervisors also support, encourage, and befriend us.

c. As God's grace grows in our lives through the working of the Holy Spirit, our conscience better enables us to recognize those courses of action which are best in line with our desire to live our lives for Him who died for us and rose again.

In a Dog-Eat-Dog World

React and Respond

1. Christ's power can be defined as a desire and ability to serve. In opposition to the natural human inclination to be served by others, Jesus took our place and in obedience to God did everything to earn our salvation for us. As Christ gives

His strength to us, He brings us to a realization of our inability to function on our own. Only by relying on Him can we be strong.

2. As the Holy Spirit works in the lives of men of God, he brings to us a desire to place the needs and concerns of others—superiors, co-workers, clients, and customers ahead of our own. This is the force of God reaching out to work good for the benefit of others in a self-focused, self-serving world.

3. Through the submission of Paul and Silas to the authority under which they had been placed, they were able to share the Gospel with the man responsible for holding them captive and his whole family. As the result of their efforts, God brought this man from the brink of suicide to the joy of salvation.

To Serve God in Serving Others

React and Respond

1a. We serve God by being conscientious employees who approach our work tasks as opportunities for service to God, undertaken for the benefit of others redeemed by Christ and done to the glory and praise of Him who died for us and rose again.

b. Many New Testament believers were slaves functioning in the social system of the day. God's Word as directed to slaves can readily be applied to all who work in reporting relationships to others. When we please our superiors, we open the door for opportunities to tell them about Jesus.

c. Even as we serve those who are unappreciative, demanding, and demeaning, or even cruel toward us, we are also serving Christ.

2. A special bond exists between believers who work together. Paul cautions that this relationship would be taken advantage of and encourages workers to treat believing superiors with extra respect and appreciation.

3a. We serve God by serving those over whom we have responsibility and authority.

b. Job's words remind us that although superiors and subordinates have much in common, superiors are answerable to God for the treatment of those placed under them.

c. God desires believing employers to treat all who work for them—believers and unbelievers alike, fairly without taking advantage of their position of authority over them.

d. Those in authority over others influence them by their

words, actions, and deeds. The Holy Spirit working through God's Word enables us to set a godly example for those under our authority.

I'vE Got You ... undER My Skin

React and Respond

1. The love of Christ motivates and empowers believers to love and forgive others.

2. Jesus gives us a set of helpful guidelines to follow in dealing with those who have wronged us. The steps include, go to the person first to resolve the problem without involving others, if the issue remains unresolved, go to the person again together with one or two others; and if the issue still remains unresolved, appeal to a still higher authority—in the case of believers, to the church.

To BrinQ HomE tHE Bacon

God ProvidEs

React and Respond

1. Accept participants' responses. Most will probably agree that, generally speaking, men tend to base their sense of who they are on what they do for a living rather than on their family and relationships. Participants will probably list the following as those most likely to suffer most from loss of employment: persons with the greatest amount of debt, those with the largest number of dependents and corresponding financial commitments, persons for whom their work is their whole life, persons without God.

2. Accept participants' responses but encourage them to provide supporting responses. Comment that God promises to take care of His own and invites us not to worry but rather to trust in Him. Ask if there is anyone who has experienced a time when he feared for his job. Ask how they handled it and what the eventual outcome was. Retrospectively, explore ways God brought good from the situation.

3a. God will provide for us. Like Jehoshaphat, we need only turn our eyes to God at all times but especially when "we do not know what to do." God works most powerfully in our lives when we admit our powerlessness. Jesus words to Paul apply also to us, "My grace is sufficient for you, for My power is made perfect in weakness" (2 Corinthians 12:9).

b. Key words and phrases for the financial struggles and challenges we face may include, "Do not be afraid or discouraged. ... For the battle is not yours, but God's. ... Stand firm and see the deliverance the LORD will give you ... Do not be afraid; do not be discouraged. Go out to face them tomorrow, and the LORD will be with you."

4. Encourage participants to identify a stressor and privately turn their concern over to God in prayer, confident of His desire to carry the burden and to work in all things for the good of those who love Him. Mention that God remains in control even when things *seem* to indicate otherwise. Only God sees the whole picture; we see only a part of it. Many men have lost their positions and struggled with a time of unemployment only to look back on this time as a new and positive change of direction for their lives.

5. Encourage participants to share their responses. Point out that God planned for work to be enjoyable and fulfilling. The difficulties and problems associated with work all result from the fall into sin.

I CAN HANDLE This

React and Respond

1. Encourage participants to share examples of the influence of false gods currently in the news or in participants' lives.

2. Accept participants' responses. Being rich toward God involves giving God our first allegiance. Point out that being rich toward God does not necessarily mean shunning worldly wealth. Many of the heroic men of faith were also blessed with abundant wealth. Comment that Jesus' parable warns about the sin of greed and of allowing financial concerns to gain a position of dominance in the lives of God's people.

3. Either having too much or too little by way of financial resources can lead to the preoccupation with money. Encourage participants to share, comparing their spiritual struggles during lean times with times of plenty.

4. The accomplishments and blessings God gives us provide us an opportunity to thank and praise Him before others for the powerful work He has done and continues to do in our lives through Jesus Christ. Similarly, Paul and Barnabas

quickly gave credit for the miracle to God and began talking about Him and His love.

5. Encourage participants to share about God's power demonstrated in their lives.

UNDER NEW MANAGEMENT
React and Respond

1a. The widow gave everything to God because she was motivated by God's great love for her. Jesus gave everything for us—including His very life.

b. Those who possess great wealth also possess the resources to do great things for the kingdom of God, using God's blessings to bring the Gospel to those without faith.

2a. Accept participants' responses on the reasons for joyful giving found in the 2 Corinthians 9 passage. Possibilities include: God loves a cheerful giver; He is able to make all grace abound to you so that in all times, having all you need you will abound in every good work; His righteousness endures forever; He ... will enlarge the harvest of your righteousness; You will be made rich in every way so that you can be generous on every occasion, through us your generosity will result in thanksgiving to God; this service that you perform is not only supplying the needs of God's people but is also overflowing in many expressions of thanks to God; men will praise God for the obedience that accompanies your confession of the Gospel and for your generosity; in their prayers for you their hearts will go out to you because of the surpassing grace God has given you; His indescribable gift.

b. God gave first to us. His gift of forgiveness, life, and salvation through Jesus motivates the giving by those who belong to Him in faith.

OPPORTUNITIES AND ADVENTURES
React and Respond

1. Accept participants' responses. Refer to Luther's conversation with his wife on the subject of generous giving to get the conversation going.

2. Paul found contentment and strength in God's love for him through Christ Jesus our Lord. Encourage participants to share about the role they desire God to have in their life's financial goals and ambitions.

93

Can You Spare Some Change?

Letters to Mom

React and Respond

1. Answers will vary. Many young men at this stage of life are optimistic about the future and anxious to be good husbands and fathers.

2. God provides the only solid foundation upon which to build life's hopes, dreams, and aspirations.

3. Life events and the corresponding changes they so often bring often make people receptive to receiving help, direction, and encouragement from new sources.

4a. Charles writes that he thanks God for his successes, though he continually credits himself for the person he has become and writes playfully if not irreverently about God and His answering of prayer.

b. Charles seems concerned about Laura, yet work concerns obviously receive more of his attention than she does.

c. Charles loves his son Timmy, although his references to Timmy sound similar to his reflections on his other accomplishments.

d. Charles' defines himself by his work.

e. Charles loves and respects his mother. He seems to distance himself from his father, preferring to relate to him through his mother.

5. Like God's Old Testament people in times of prosperity, when we become comfortable in life, we may come to put our faith and trust in ourselves, in our property, and in our accomplishment rather than in the God who has so graciously given us all things.

6. God continually calls us to repent of our sins, to receive the forgiveness Jesus earned for us at Calvary and to return to the new life He has given us to live for Him.

7. Charles sees God as the one who either brought him trouble or refused to keep trouble away from him.

8. Although Charles asks for help (any help he can get), he still seems confident in his own ability to handle things on his own.

9. Jesus desires all who feel the burden of sin and its consequences in their lives to come to Him for forgiveness, restoration, and strength.

10. Charles could follow the Spirit's leading in His life and repent and turn his life over to God and His leading. Or, Charles could resist God's desire for him and continue in the hold darkness and despair have upon his life.

11. Jesus refreshes those who repent with His love and forgiveness.

12a. God will give all who love and trust in Him all things—including wealth, reward, and pleasure—either in this life or in the life to come.

b. God helps His people find their strength and identity in Him.

c. God makes His followers comfortable and content in the knowledge that they are loved and cared for by Him.

New Beginnings
React and Respond

1. Answers will vary.

2. God gives to us the power to remain under His loving care and guidance through His Word as we read and study it and as we receive it together at His Table in the company of other believers.

3a. Peter reminds us that God's people will never find ready acceptance in the prevailing worldview of our fallen world. He encourages us to consider ourselves, in effect, a counter-culture movement.

b. We can approach life's changes and challenges with confidence knowing that Jesus is greater than any opposition.

Facing Change
React and Respond

1. Answers will vary.

2. Answers will vary.

3. We don't always know why specific hardships and setbacks befall us, but we can be confident that when trouble comes our way, God's tear is the first to fall. He has promised to work all things for our good (Romans 8:28) so that Jesus' honor and glory may be revealed.

God at Work
React and Respond

1. Jesus will give us all we need to sustain us in our saving relationship with Him.

2. Jesus nourishes and sustains us physically through His generous daily provisions and spiritually through His Word.

3. When we live our lives for God, we honor and glorify His name. We ask for the ability to do this when we pray the Lord's Prayer.

4. Every appropriate Christian philosophy of life involves keeping our focus on Jesus, the author and perfecter of our faith.

5. Our great and loving God is able to do for all His sons immeasurably more than all we ask or imagine. And He will do it!